Landscapes of
TENERIFE

a countryside guide
Seventh edition

Noel Rochford

SUNFLOWER BOOKS

For Ramona

Seventh edition © 2007
Sunflower Books™
PO Box 36160
London SW7 3WS, UK
www.sunflowerbooks.co.uk

Published in the USA by
Hunter Publishing Inc
130 Campus Drive
Edison, NJ 08818
www.hunterpublishing.com

ISBN 978-1-85691-337-9

Cave houses (Walk 25)

Important note to the reader

We have tried to ensure that the descriptions and maps in this book are error-free at press date. The book will be updated, where necessary, whenever future printings permit. It will be very helpful for us to receive your comments (sent in care of the publishers, please) for the updating of future printings.

We also rely on those who use this book — especially walkers — to take along a good supply of common sense when they explore. Conditions change fairly rapidly on Tenerife, and **storm damage or bulldozing may make a route unsafe at any time**. If the route is not as we outline it here, and your way ahead is not secure, return to the point of departure. **Never attempt to complete a tour or walk under hazardous conditions!** Please read carefully the notes on pages 33-40, and the introductory comments at the beginning of each tour and walk (regarding road conditions, equipment, grade, distances and time, etc). Explore **safely**, while at the same time respecting the beauty of the countryside.

Cover photograph: El Teide covered in snow
Title page: mural at Teno Alto (Car tour 3, Walk 20)

Photographs: the author, except for pages 22, 23, 26, 27, 32-3, 42-3, 51, 67, 89, 111, 112 (Andreas Stieglitz), 102 (Conny Spelbrink), and cover (istock-photo)
Maps: John Underwood, based on the 1:25,000 maps of the Servicio Geográfico del Ejército
Drawings: Sharon Rochford
A CIP catalogue record for this book is available from the British Library.
Printed and bound in England: J H Haynes & Co Ltd

10 9 8 7 6 5 4 3 2 1

❀ Contents

4   Landscapes of Tenerife

# Preface

Tenerife has something for everyone — country lanes for strolling, nature trails for hiking, mountains to be scaled, and beaches where you can while away the day.

To absorb the island's beauty takes time. Her personality lies in the countryside, and her moods are captured at sunrise and sunset. The bleak south is a mystery of dry terraced slopes, sliced through by deep ravines. The lush and green northern escarpment yields up forested hillsides rolling off the central massif, soon burgeoning with produce as it steps its way down to an indigo sea. Las Cañadas, the focal point of every visit, lies embedded in the island's backbone. Pine-studded slopes lead you up to this world apart, where strange hues and tormented rock forms are dominated by the majesty of El Teide.

In spring the island is a living tapestry of colour. This is the best time for exploring. The profusion of wild plants and flowers makes the island a botanical treasure. But no season is without its bloom and pot-pourri of colour.

Over the last few years Tenerife has become a mecca for hikers, with generally well-marked trails criss-crossing her incredible kaleidoscope of landscapes. The Anaga — spectaclar coastal scenery, and laurel forests dripping with lichen and cushioned in moss; Las Cañadas — the unforgettable moonscape; Teno — a hidden world of tilting plateaus and deep chasms; the Oratava Valley — a lush chequerboard of fields and gardens embraced by pines.

But you needn't be a walker to appreciate Tenerife's beauty. The car tours, with their encompassing panoramas, will give you a taste of the landscapes. The picnic spots will, I hope, encourage you to meander just a little further off the beaten track. Then there are several short walks that require no great expenditure of energy and make a memorable day's outing.

My love for Tenerife led me into the depths of the countryside in the early 1980s. My short strolls soon turned into longer rambles and these, in turn, became long hikes. I'd become an avid walker and explorer. The fact that I saw so few other walkers prompted me to write the first edition of this book — to encourage you to step off the usual touring routes, to see and feel the real Tenerife. There's an unending source of weird and wonderful countryside just awaiting your exploration, and I hope that *Landscapes of Tenerife* will help you find it.

Mass tourism, especially over the last decade, has brought the island both benefits and disadvantages. The people have seen their Shangri-La undergo a great transformation, much of it unwelcomed. They are gradually losing great tracts of land to foreigners, who have no interest in being part of island life. This has dampened the natural Canarian warmth and friendliness, but it has not yet vanished altogether. A few words of Spanish and a friendly smile of greeting will help, but I cannot recommend too strongly that you pick up at least a smattering of Spanish — this will make all the difference between having a good holiday and a truly memorable one.

Acknowledgements

I would like to express my gratitude to the following organisations and people, who helped with the preparation of the original edition of thi book:

For maps and general information: ICONA; the Delegación del Ministerio de Comercio y Turismo; local government offices (Cabildo) and the Department of Public Works in Santa Cruz; the Servicio Geográfico del Ejército in Madrid.

For guiding and advice: The Grupo Montañero de Tenerife for information, especially Edmundo Herrero Rello and Rafael Valencia.

My sister, Sharon, for her splendid drawings.

Finally, very special thanks to Conny Spelbrink, who has completely updated this edition. Conny, in turn, would like to thank three beautiful hotels where she stayed during her research: the Hotel San Roque in Garachico (www.hotelsanroque.com), the Hotel Costa Salada in Valle de Guerra (on the Anaga coast north of Tacoronte; www.costasalada.com), and the Hotel Rural Caserío Los Partidos (en route in Walk 16; www.caserío-lospartidos.com).

Useful books

Be sure to pack a good standard guide to Tenerife. During your visit, you might like to look for the following books, all of which are available on the island.

Bramwell, D, and Bramwell, Z *Wild Flowers of the Canary Islands,* London, Stanley Thornes

Cano, D M *Tenerife,* León, Editorial Everest

Cuscoy, L D and Larsen, P C *The Book of Tenerife,* Santa Cruz de Tenerife, Instituto de Estudios Canarios

Also available from Sunflower (by Noel Rochford)
  Landscapes of Fuerteventura
  Landscapes of Gran Canaria
  Landscapes of La Palma and El Hierro
  Landscapes of Lanzarote
  Landscapes of Southern Tenerife and La Gomera

Candelaria (Car tour 5)

Getting about

There is no doubt that a **hired car** is the most convenient way of getting about Tenerife, and car rental on the island is extremely good value, especially if you shop around.

The second most flexible form of transport is a hired **taxi** and, especially if three or four people are sharing the cost, this becomes an attractive idea. If you're making an unmetered journey, do agree on the price *before* setting out: all taxi drivers should carry an official price list.

Coach tours are the most popular way of seeing many holiday islands; this is an easy way to get to know a place in comfort, before embarking on your own adventures.

My favourite way of getting about is by **local bus.** The system is very economical and reliable. The plans on the following two pages show you where to board buses in Puerto de la Cruz and Santa Cruz, as well as the Santa Cruz/La Laguna tram. On pages 136-140 you will find timetables for all the buses used for the walks and picnics in this book. But please do not rely *solely* on these timetables. Pick up the latest bus timetables from the nearest bus station or, better still, from the station in Santa Cruz (the most ample and up-to-date). It always pays to verify bus departures and returns for long journeys and less frequent services *before* setting out, and it always pays to arrive a bit *early!* The local bus company is called TITSA. They operate a very efficient web site (www.titsa.com), from which you can download all the latest timetables and route maps before you visit the island. If you plan to make good use of the buses, be sure to buy a fare-saver 'TITSA-Bono' bus card when you arrive.

PUERTO DE LA CRUZ

1 Town hall (Ayuntamiento) and Tourist information
2 Castillo de San Felipe
3 Plaza Viera y Clavijo
4 Post office
5 Nuestra Señora de la Peña
6 Hotel Semiramis
7 Casino Taoro
8 Bull ring
9 Bus station
10 Hospital/24-hour first aid
11 Mirador de la Paz
12 Puerto Pesquero
13 Casa Iriarte
14 Mirador de la Costa
city exits
Exit A leads to the TF320 to Icod and the TF5 westbound
Exit B leads to the motorway (TF5) to La Laguna and Santa Cruz

SANTA CRUZ

1 Plaza de España
2 Cabildo (local government headquarters), Tourist information, Archaeological museum
3 Post office
4 San Francisco church
5 Municipal museum of fine arts
6 Market
7 Bus station
8 Plaza General Weyler
9 Tramline (goes to La Laguna)
city exits
Exit A (Avenida 3 de Mayo) leads to the motorways north (TF5) and south (TF1)
Exit B (Avenida de Anaga) leads to San Andrés and the northern Anaga via El Bailadero

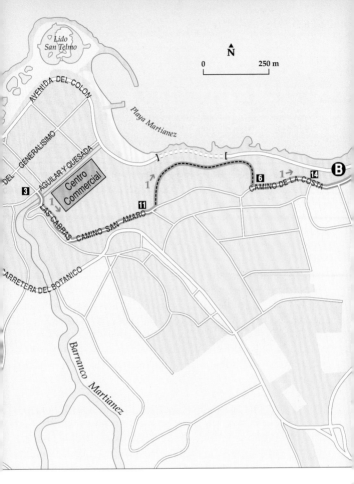

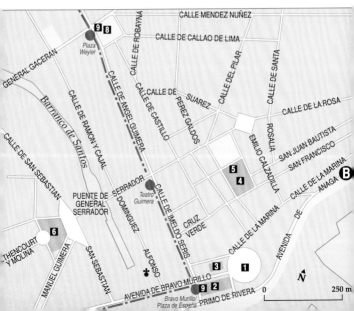

☀ Picnicking

Picnickers are extremely well catered for on Tenerife. Medio Ambiente (the nature conservation agency) and the island government have worked together to set up several very well-equipped 'recreation areas' around the island. At these *zonas recreativas* (which tend to be crowded on weekends and holidays), you'll find tables and benches, barbecues, WCs, drinking fountains and play areas for children. They've also scattered simple little wooden shelters, with tables and benches, in some of the island's loveliest settings. You'll find many of these *chozas* along the TF21 (the 'Las Cañadas road') and in the Orotava Valley.

All **roadside** picnic areas **with tables** (and sometimes other facilities) are indicated both in the car touring notes and on the touring and walking maps by the symbol ⊼. They are also briefly described on the following pages, together with suggestions for picnics 'off the beaten track'.

All the information you need to get to any of the suggested picnic spots is given on the following pages. *Picnic numbers correspond to walk numbers,* so you can quickly find the general location on the island by looking at the touring map inside the back cover, where the walks are numbered in green. I give transport details (🚐: bus numbers; 🚗: where to park), walking times, and views or setting. Beside the picnic title, you'll find a map reference: the exact location of the picnic spot is shown on this *walking map* by the symbol **P**, printed in green.

Please glance over the comments *before* you set off: if some walking is involved, remember to wear sensible shoes and to **take a sunhat** (○ indicates a picnic in **full sun**). It's a good idea to take along a plastic groundsheet as well, in case the ground is damp or prickly.

If you are travelling to your picnic by bus, be sure to arm yourself with up-to-date bus timetables (see page 7). **If you are travelling to your picnic by car**, be extra vigilant off the main roads: children and animals are often in the village streets. Without damaging plants, do park *well off* the road; **never** block a road or track. **All picnickers should read the country code on page 39 and go quietly in the countryside.**

3 CHOZA CHIMOCHE (map pages 54-55, photograph page 47)

by car or taxi: 45min on foot   *by bus: 45min on foot*

🚐 either at the Bermeja picnic area or at the Choza Chimoche turn-off, at the beginning of the track (both are on the TF21, about 5km south of Aguamansa; see map pages 54-55). Car tour 1

🚌 348: ask to be put off at 'Choza Bermeja'.

Walk east on the forestry track just south of the Bermeja *choza*. You'll come to Choza Chimoche after a gentle climb of about 45 minutes. A few minutes past here is another picnic spot, at the mouth of a dry *barranco* (the Barranco de los Llanos. Shade.

5 CHOZA EL TOPO (map pages 54-55)

by car or taxi: 1h on foot   *by bus: 1h on foot*

🚐 La Caldera car park (TF21). Car tour 1   🚌 345 to La Caldera

Follow Short walk 5 (page 49). There's a slight ascent. Views over Agua-mansa's valley. Shade.

Montaña de las Arenas, from the main road at
La Crucita (Car tour 5, Walk 7, Picnic 7)

6a LA CALDERA (map pages 54-55) ⊼

by car or taxi: up to 5min on foot   *by bus: up to 5min on foot*
🚘 La Caldera car park (TF21). Car tour 1   🚌 345 to La Caldera
Zona recreativa with full facilities (see page 10). Views over the Orotava Valley.

6b ABOVE CHOZA PEREZ VENTOSO (map pages 54-55)

by car or taxi: 30-40min on foot   *by bus: 30-40min on foot*
🚘 trout farm car park or the bar/restaurant just north of the trout farm (TF21, just south of Aguamansa). Car tour 1
🚌 345 to Aguamansa
Follow the TF21 downhill: 100m/yds below the bar/restaurant turn right off the TF21 (the Aguamansa bus shelter will be on your left as you turn). A few minutes downhill, take the first right turn (for 'Mamio, Pinoleris, and La Florida'). Follow this tarred lane for 15-20 minutes, then keep left at a junction, towards Pinoleris. After 200m/yds come to a shrine on the right; turn right on the narrow road just beyond it. The tar ends at the ruined Choza Perez Ventoso. Take the track to the left here, climbing steeply to a *new choza* about 5-6 minutes uphill. Shade.

7 LA CRUCITA (map pages 54-55, photograph page 11)

by car or taxi: 5-30min on foot   *by bus: not easily accessible*
🚘 off the side of the TF24 at La Crucita, 13km east of El Portillo (signposted). Car tour 5
Picnic by the side of the track, or explore either side of the TF24. If you go west, you'll have views of the Orotava Valley and El Teide; to the east you would overlook Montaña de las Arenas (see text on page 59). Shade. *Note that these descents are steep and slippery.*

8a CHOZA MONTAÑA DEL ALTO (map pages 62-63)

by car or taxi: up to 5min on foot   *by bus: 15-20min on foot*
🚘 at Montaña del Alto. Car tours 1, 5   🚌 348 to El Portillo
From El Portillo head east on the TF24: the *choza* can be seen on the north side of the road after 1km. Views of El Teide. Shade at the shelter.

8b-g LAS CAÑADAS ROAD (touring map) ⊼

There are six *chozas* on the TF21 (the 'Las Cañadas road'; Car tour 1) between Aguamansa and El Portillo; all are signposted with the letter 'P'. Shade.

8b Choza Bermeja: both sides of the road; shelter, tables, benches

8c Choza Wildpret: south side of the road; shelter, tables, benches

8d Zona Recreativa Ramón Caminero: both sides of the road; tables, benches, barbecues, camping

8e Galería Pino de la Cruz: south side of road; shelter

8f Choza Bethencourt: north side of the road; shelter

8g Choza Sventenius: north side of the road; shelter

Margarita de Piedra (above) and Margarita del Teide (Argytanthemum antethifolium)

11 LOS ROQUES DE GARCIA (map pages 68-69, photographs pages 71, 73) ○

by car or taxi: 15-30min on foot
by bus: 15-30min on foot
🚘 at the Los Roques car park (on the west side of the TF21, near the Parador). Car tour 1
🚌 348 to the Parador de las Cañadas

Follow Walk 11 for a short time, or just amble about until you find a comfortable rock. Marvellous views of El Teide, Guajara and the weird rock formations, but the only shade is from the rocks themselves.

12 PIEDRAS AMARILLAS (map pages 68-69, photograph page 19) ○

by car or taxi: 15-30min on foot   *by bus: 15-30min on foot*
🚗 at the Parador. Car tour 1   🚌 348 to the Parador
Follow Walk 12 (page 74) to the 'Yellow Stones'. Always crowded. No shade.

13a CHANAJIGA (map page 77) 🛱

by car or taxi: up to 5min on foot   *by bus: not easily accessible*
🚗 Chanajiga car park: head south from La Orotava on the TF21, and after 9km turn right on the TF326 (just past Mirador Brisas; signposted towards Benijos). Then take the signposted turn-off for Chanajiga at Las Llanadas. Near Car tour 1
Zona recreativa with full facilities (see page 10). Note that a lot of forestry work is going on in this area.

13b CAÑADA DE LOS GUANCHEROS (map page 77, photographs page 78) ○

by car or taxi: 15-55min on foot   *by bus: 15-55min on foot*
🚗 Las Cañadas Visitors' Centre (TF21 near El Portillo). Car tours 1, 5
🚌 348 to El Portillo
Follow Walk 13 (page 77) to picnic along the path (bottom photograph page 77; 15min), or walk on to the *cañada* (55min; near the top two photographs). Limited shade.

14 LA CORONA (map pages 84-85) ○

by car or taxi: up to 5min on foot   *by bus: 50min on foot*
🚗 at the La Corona *mirador*. From Icod el Alto, continue west on the TF342 towards La Guancha. Take the first tarred turn-off left (signposted), about five minutes west of Icod. Near Car tour 3
🚌 354 to Icod el Alto; then follow Walk 14 (page 80) — a very steep climb of 250m/800ft.
Overlooks the entire Orotava Valley to the eastern escarpment. Little shade.

15 EL LAGAR (map pages 84-85) 🛱

by car or taxi: up to 5min on foot   *by bus: not easily accessible*
🚗 at El Lagar: head west for La Guancha on the TF342. In the town, take the first turning left, just past the petrol station. From here on, the way to El Lagar is signposted. If approaching La Guancha from the west, take a right turn just *before* the petrol station. Car tour 3
Large *zona recreativa* (see page 10) in the shade of pines.

16 LAS ARENAS NEGRAS (map pages 90-91, photograph page 89) 🛱

by car or taxi: 1h on foot   *by bus: 1h on foot*
🚗 car park at La Montañeta. The TF336 climbs the slopes above Icod de los Vinos to join the TF82 above Erjos. La Montañeta lies halfway up this road. Park at the roadside chapel above La Montañeta. The local people drive up the rough track all the way to the picnic grounds, but this is not recommended with a hired car, since you are not likely to be insured for damage to tyres. Car tour 3
🚌 363 to Icod de los Vinos and 🚌 360 from Icod to La Montañeta
Follow Walk 16 (page 88) to Las Arenas Negras, a steep climb of 250m/800ft. Shade of pines and full *zona recreativa* facilities (see page

10). Busy on weekends: to get away from the crowd, continue uphill past the picnic grounds for another 10-20 minutes.

17 NEAR ERJOS (map pages 90-91) ○

by car or taxi: 10-55min on foot   *by bus: 10-55min on foot*
🚐 at Erjos (TF82, between El Tanque and Santiago). Car tour 3
🚌 325 to Erjos
Follow Walk 17 (page 93) as far as you like. Soon there are views to El Teide, and you can picnic beside the track. Gentle climb back to your transport. Not recommended on weekends.

18a PUERTO DE ERJOS (map pages 90-91) ○

by car or taxi: 10-15min on foot   *by bus 10-20min on foot*
🚐 in a lay-by on the south side of the pass: there are two lay-bys within 200m of the pass, on the TF82, 3km north of Santiago del Teide.
🚌 325 to Erjos: get off at Puerto de Erjos
Walk as far as you like up the narrow road that climbs to summit of Montaña Jala and choose an appealing spot (the landscapes on either side of the ridge are quite different). A 40 minute climb would take you to the summit — for a spectacular view over the northwest corner of the island. Limited shade off the side of the road.

18b THE PONDS NEAR PUERTO DE ERJOS (map pages 90-91, photograph page 97) ○

by car or taxi: 10-20min on foot   *by bus 10-20min on foot*
🚐 Restaurante Fleytas, 2km south of Erjos on TF82.
🚌 325 to Erjos: get off at Restaurante Fleytas, above Erjos
Follow Walk 18 (page 95) to the lush herbaceous basin with its pretty ponds, visible from roadside above. No shade.

19a LA TABAIBA PASS (map pages 100-101) ○

by car or taxi: 5-15min on foot   *by bus: 5-15min on foot*
🚐 at La Tabaiba Pass (*not* signposted); it's the highest point on the TF436 south of Las Portelas, before the road descends to Masca.
🚌 363, then 🚌 366 (see Walk 19, page 98)
Follow the path from the *mirador* and parking area, to climb the ridge (Cumbres de Baracán) as far as you like. There are fine views of the El Palmar Valley and the ravine of El Carrizal. Limited shade.

19b LA SIETE (map pages 100-101, photograph page 99) ○

by car or taxi: 10-20min on foot   *by bus not accessible.*
🚐 well off the end of the road in the hamlet of La Siete, 1km above Teno Alto. To get there, take the narrow road that ascends steeply to the left from Teno Alto, passing the bodega/village shop immediately.
Walk along the track that continues straight off the road. In a few minutes you're looking into a deep valley. Head up to the right, to a natural hillside balcony and enjoy one of the best spots on the island, especially in spring, with views to El Teide and the hidden corners of Teno. Limited shade nearby.

20 PUNTA DE TENO (map pages 100-101, photograph page 28) ○

by car or taxi: up to 10min on foot   *by bus: not accessible*
🚐 at Punta de Teno, 8km from Buenavista (TF445). Car tour 3
Exquisite views of sea cliffs and the lava promontory at the lighthouse. The only shade is from the cliffs.

22 BATAN DE ABAJO (map on reverse of touring map) ○

by car or taxi: 10-15min on foot   *by bus 10-15min on foot*
🚗 village car park, below Batán de Abajo. Turn off the TF12 0.8km west of Cruz del Carmen; keep right all the way to Batán de Abajo.
🚌 074 to Batán de Abajo; the bus stop is at the village car park.
Walk uphill from the car park, then take the first left. Just past the village bar, turn right along an alley, signposted for Punta del Hidalgo. Walk to the second ridge, some 10 minutes away. Superb views over this vast valley and its adjoining ridges, as well as the Barranco del Tomadero. No immediate shade.

23a PLAYA DE LOS TROCHES (map on reverse of touring map) ○

by car or taxi: 10-15min on foot   *by bus: 10-15min on foot*
🚗 turning circle at the end of the TF13, beyond Punta del Hidalgo. Car tour 4
🚌 105 to Punta del Hidalgo
Follow Walk 23 (page 111) to this stony beach. Steep descent and ascent. The only shade is from the cliffs.

23b LAS ESCALERAS (map on reverse of touring map)

by car or taxi: 25-35min on foot   *by bus: 25-35min on foot*
🚗 Las Carboneras: turn off the TF12 1km east of Cruz del Carmen. Then keep left for Las Carboneras. Car tour 4
🚌 075 to Las Carboneras
Follow *Alternative walk* 23 (page 111) to Las Escaleras, a viewpoint overlooking two valleys. Easy climb and descent of 100m/330ft. Shade nearby.

23c MIRADOR ERA DE LAS ALMACIGAS
(map on reverse of touring map, nearby photograph page 112) ○

by car or taxi: 15-20min on foot   *by bus: not accessible*
🚗 Chinamada: follow 23b above, then continue past Las Carboneras to Chinamada, at the end of the TF145.
From the plaza in Chinamada, walk behind the church and follow the signposted path to the *mirador.* Superb coastal views and outlook over Punta del Hidalgo. No shade.

24 NEAR TABORNO (map on reverse of touring map,
photographs pages 30, 116, 126) ○

by car or taxi: 25-30min on foot   *by bus: 25-30min on foot*
🚗 Taborno: turn off the TF12 1km east of Cruz del Carmen. Then keep right for Taborno. Car tour 4
🚌 075 to Taborno
Follow Walk 24 from Taborno (page 114) to the top of the ridge reached in 30min. No shade.

25 AFUR (map on reverse of touring map, photograph page 119) ○

by car or taxi: 15-20min on foot   *by bus: 15-20min on foot*
🚗 Afur: the turn-off is under 2km east of the turn-off to Pico del Inglés.
🚌 076 to Afur (see notes for *Short walk 2* on page 117)
Follow Walk 25 from Afur (page 118) to the big balancing rock. Quiet spot overlooking a winding barranco. The only shade is from the rock.

26 BARRANCO DE TAHODIO (map on reverse of touring map,
photograph page 122)

by car or taxi: 20-30min on foot   *by bus: 30-40min on foot*
🚗 Mirador Pico del Inglés. Car tours 2, 4
🚌 075, 076 or 077 to the Pico del Inglés turn-off

Follow Walk 26 (page 121) to the lookout point over the *barranco* and dam. There are also views to El Teide. Tiring climb to return. Shade.

28a ANAGA FORESTRY PARK (map on reverse of touring map)

by car or taxi: up to 5min on foot   *by bus: up to 5min on foot*
🚗 forestry park, on the TF123, east of El Bailadero, before the KM5 road marker. Car tour 2. Or 🚌
Picnic in the shade of laurels — or follow Walk 28 from here to Chinobre — one of the best viewpoints on Tenerife (see page 128).

28b PLAYA DE BENIJO (map on reverse of touring map) ○

by car or taxi: up to 5min on foot   *by bus: 10-15min on foot*
🚗 near the beach, 4km past Taganana on the TF134. Car tour 2
🚌 246; ask to be put off at the Almáciga turn-off and walk east to the beach, a few minutes away.
Beautiful coastal views. The coast at nearby Almáciga is shown on page 22. No shade.

29 CHAMORGA OVERLOOK (map on reverse of touring map) ○

by car or taxi: 15-20min on foot   *by bus: 15-20min on foot*
🚗 Chamorga: at the end of the TF123, the 71km-point in Car tour 2
🚌 247 from Santa Cruz to Chamorga at 07.30 *Sat only*; returns 15.00, 18.00
The road ends just below a bar/shop. From here follow a path up behind and to the left of the bar and toilets, to the top of the ridge overlooking the village and its ravine. No shade. Steep, short climb of about 100m/ 330ft. Possibility of vertigo. Fine view back over the village and across the valley.

30a IGUESTE (map on reverse of touring map) ○

by car or taxi: 5-10min on foot   *by bus: 5-10min on foot*
🚗 Igueste, at the end of the TF121. Car tour 2   🚌 245 to Igueste
Follow Walk 30 (page 132) but, where main walk bears left up Pasate Julio, descend to the right, to the stony beach — a pleasant spot with fine coastal views, but no shade. Photo of Igueste page 133.

30b LAS CASILLAS (map on reverse of touring map, photograph left) ○

by car or taxi: 30-40min on foot
by bus: 30-40min on foot
🚗 off the TF123: about 10km east of El Bailadero, on a sharp bend in the road, there should be a small yellow sign for 'Igueste' on the right, pointing down a path. Beside the path, a road turns off to the right: park at the side of this road. Car tour 2
🚌 247 (not Sundays; see notes for *Short walk 2* on page 132)
Follow Short walk 2 on page 132 to Las Casillas. Shade nearby.

Las Casillas (Picnic 30b)

# Touring

Car hire on the island is extremely good value. *Do* shop around; hire prices vary considerably. Examine the car before you take it on the road, and make certain that the applicable motoring laws and insurance information are given to you in writing *in English*.

The car tours are numbered in order of importance: if you will only tour for a day or two, there is no question about priorities. Don't miss Tour 1! If you don't mind a long day's touring, you can combine Car tours 2 and 4.

The touring notes are brief: they include little history or information readily available in standard guides or in free leaflets obtainable from the tourist offices. The facilities and 'sights' of the towns are not described for this same reason. Instead, I concentrate on the 'logistics' of touring: times and distances, road conditions, and seeing some of 'hidden' Tenerife. Most of all, I emphasise possibilities for **walking** and **picnicking** (the symbol *P* alerts you to a picnic spot; see pages 10-16). While some of the references to picnics 'off the beaten track' may not be suitable during a long car tour, you may see a landscape that you would like to explore at leisure another day, when you have more time.

The large touring map can be opened opposite the touring notes and contains all the information you will need outside the towns. The tours have been written up with Puerto as departure/return point, but can easily be joined from other centres. Plans of Puerto de la Cruz and Santa Cruz, with city exits, are on pages 8 and 9.

Take along warm clothing and some **food and drink**: you may experience delays, especially on mountainous roads. **Allow plenty of time for stops**: the times given for the tours include only brief stops at viewpoints labelled (☎) in the notes. **Telephones** are located in most villages. WC is used to indicate public toilets; others are found at restaurants.

Distances quoted are *cumulative km **from Puerto.*** A key to the symbols in the touring notes is on the touring map.

All motorists should read the country code on page 39 and go quietly in the countryside. *Buen viaje!*

17

1 THE OROTAVA VALLEY AND LAS CAÑADAS

Puerto de la Cruz • La Orotava • Las Cañadas • Los Gigantes • Guía de Isora • Adeje • Playa de las Américas • Playa de los Cristianos • Vilaflor • Las Cañadas • Puerto de la Cruz

239km/148mi; 7-8h driving; Exit B from Puerto (plan pages 8-9)

En route: 🚂 at La Caldera, Montaña del Alto, Las Cañadas road, Chio, Las Lajas; Picnics (see **P** symbol and pages 10-16): 3, 5, 6a, 6b, 8a-g, 11, 12, (13a), 13b; Walks 1-13

This long excursion requires a very early start. *Don't be put off by dark clouds over the north, because very often Las Cañadas and the south are soaking up the sunshine! All roads are in good condition.*

This dramatic circuit begins gently, in the lush Orotava Valley. We wind our way up into the pines on the higher slopes and soon the landscape changes abruptly: we cross the vast, bare plateau of the Las Cañadas crater. Fields of jagged scoria layer the floor with the occasional sprinkling of *retama*, a hardy broom. Southward, heading towards the coast, some calmness returns to the landscape, as smooth mounds of the more recent volcanoes emerge. Picturesque villages set on the severe southern escarpments remind us of the other side of Tenerife — a more sombre beauty.

Leave Puerto via the Carretera del Este (Avenida de Colón), then follow the TF21 through **La Orotava★** (7km ✝🏔✕🚐⊕M).* The road (🚐✕) continues uphill past the turn-off to Benijos (15km 📷✕; **P**13a with 🚂 at Chanagjiga). Old lichen-covered walls hide well-tilled plots, and scatterings of aged chestnut trees line the route to **Aguamansa** and the **trout farm** (20km ✕wc**P**6b), where Walks 2-4 begin and Walk 6 ends. Just after, turn left to **La Caldera★** (22km ✕🚂wc**P**5, 6a). This tiny crater, where Walks 5-7 begin and Walk 8 ends, is a superb viewpoint over the green Orotava slopes and down to the sea. From here keep climbing, past the famous Margarita de Piedra★ (📷), a rock shaped like a daisy (see page 12), and several roadside picnic areas (🚂; **P**3, 8b-g).

Walks 8, 9 and 13 begin at **El Portillo** (37km ✕**P**8a, 13b), where the nearby **Cañadas Visitors' Information**

*As this is a very long tour and La Orotava is so close to Puerto, save your visit for another day. The town is best seen during the festival of Corpus Christi (May/June): the streets are carpeted in flowers, and in the main square intriguingly-beautiful religious 'paintings' are made from the multi-coloured sands of Las Cañadas. Visit Calle de San Francisco, with its magnificent old mansions, lovely courtyards and wooden balconies. Also of interest are the main church (La Concepción, 18C, the botanical gardens, and the church of San Juan, which commands a superb view of the Orotava Valley.

Centre (*i*WC) welcomes you to 'another planet' — **Las Cañadas★**. The constant change in colour and rock formation within the encircling crater walls (photograph page 67) is the highlight of this tour — and, I imagine, of your visit. Sharp streams of rock give way to smooth mounds of pumice and fine scoria, while sunken sea-beds of gravel create 'pools' along the floor. The majestic El Teide is with you wherever you go, and Montaña de

The Piedras Amarillas (Yellow Stones) rise in front of the rumpled crown of Guajara (Walks 9 and 12; Picnic 12)

Beautifully-carved wooden ornamentation and patios bursting with greenery are features of many older Canarian homes.

Guajara, rising out of the encircling wall like an abutment, rivals El Teide in beauty.

The leisurely drive through this wonderland (⊕ and 🎦 at Minas de San José and Tabonal) takes you past the turn-off to Montaña Blanca and El Teide (Walk 10). A few kilometres beyond the cable car station (Short walk 9), you come to the **Parador de las Cañadas** (52km ▲▲✕*i* *P*12) and the **Roques de García★** (🎦*P*11), a troupe of rocky upthrusts overlooking the vast Ucanca Plain. Walks 11 and 12 begin and end here. Barely a kilometre further on, you'll be intrigued by the patches blue rock in the embankment at the side of the road ('Los Azulejos') — even more striking when seen from the plain below. Mirador Llano de Ucanca (🎦) affords yet another perspective over this setting.

At the pass of **Boca Tauce** (59km) fork right on the TF38 for 'Guía de Isora'. Pico Viejo is the prominent dark mound on the right. For several kilometres, the road cuts its way through the dark lava flows. Pines reappear, scattered across the landscape, and smooth volcanic cones remind you of the last volcanic outbursts. Set amidst this scenery is the lovely Chio *zona recreativa* (🎪). Past here, the Las Estrellas restaurant (✕🎦) is a good viewing point over the southwest coast.

At a junction (88km 🚻), leave the TF38 and continue to the right along the TF82 towards Santiago del Teide. At **Tamaimo** (93km ✕🚻), an attractive village sheltering below a high rocky protrusion, turn left on the TF454. Greenhouses for tomatoes now cover the landscape as the route winds down to Los Gigantes. At the 98km-mark, at a junction, keep right for Puerto de Santiago. **Los Gigantes** (100km ▲▲▲✕🎦) is a modern tourist complex, set against a backdrop of sheer cliffs★ rising vertically out of the sea. From Los Gigantes make for nearby **Puerto de Santiago** (▲▲▲✕🚻⊕) and the adjoining Playa de la Arena. Continue past **Alcalá** (▲✕🚻) to tranquil **San Juan** (110km ▲▲✕🚻).

From San Juan head up the TF463 towards **Guía de**

Isora (✗➡⊕), a small country town sitting on bare rock slopes. Passing below the town (120km), continue to the right on the TF82. Then turn off left to **Adeje★**, 2km off the main road (135km ▲▲▲✗). Park on the main street. The town rests below crags, and a table-topped mountain fills the background. A great chasm, the Barranco del Infierno★, runs past the edge of the village.* Adeje is also well known for its *pollo en mojo* (chicken with spicy sauce), which makes it a good spot to stop for lunch. Leaving, follow the main street back to the TF82, which takes you to the motorway towards Santa Cruz (➡).

Now you have a choice of fine sandy beaches, easily accessible from the motorway. The best known are Playa de las Américas (▲▲▲✗➡⊕WC), a lively resort with everything going 'in top gear' and Playa de los Cristianos (▲▲▲✗➡⊕WC), somewhat smaller and less frenetic.

The main tour bypasses these built-up areas, to head inland again via Arona. Take Exit 26 (the same motorway exit as for Los Cristianos). Rejoining the old TF28 (⊕ and camel park) follow it for 4.5km to a junction, then head left on the TF51 ('Aguilas del Teide' ecology park). **Arona** (150km ✚✗➡🎞) has a charming shady church square, surrounded by balconied old houses. It overlooks the sparkling greenhouses on the lowlands. Vineyards on walled slopes surround the TF51 to **Vilaflor** (164km ✚▲▲▲✗➡⊕🎞M), the highest town on Tenerife at 1161m/3810ft. Nestled on the edge of a plain, this mountain settlement looks up onto the steep, forested inclines that run down off the high mountain spurs above. From Vilaflor follow the TF21 back to Las Cañadas, passing some of the loveliest Canary pine forests on the island. Pino Gordo, a *mirador* 2km past Vilaflor, sits amidst these regal ancient pines (🎞). The road takes you through some spectacular rugged mountain landscapes (🛱 at 175km, Las Lajas *zona recreativa*.

You re-enter the crater at Boca Tauce (181km). The twisted uprising of rock here is more impressive when approached from the south. Bear right along the TF21 and return to Puerto under the late afternoon sun. The mood of Las Cañadas changes under this soft light. Shadows fall across the crater floor, colours mellow, and low clouds begin curling over the crater walls, as you retrace your outgoing route to **Puerto** (239km).

*This popular hike is described in *Landscapes of Southern Tenerife and La Gomera*.

2 THE RUGGED ANAGA PENINSULA

Puerto de la Cruz • Pico del Inglés • Roque Negro • El Bailadero • Chamorga • Taganana • Almáciga • Benijo • San Andrés • Igueste • Puerto de la Cruz

171km/106mi; 5-6h driving; Exit B from Puerto (plan pages 8-9)

En route: ⛺ at the Anaga Forestry Park, El Bailadero tunnel; Picnics (see **P** symbol and pages 10-16): (25), 26-30; Walks 24-30

*Driving is slow in this mountainous terrain, with fairly heavy tourist traffic. Fill up with petrol before starting out; there are no petrol stations in the Anaga, and none on the touring route until San Andrés. **Hint:** Beyond Las Mercedes, refer to the large-scale map of the Anaga on the reverse of the touring map.*

This excursion takes us amidst the mountains of the Anaga Peninsula. Twisting along the backbone of this range, the road is one continuous *mirador*. Inland, lost in these rugged contours, lie tiny remote villages, clinging to rocky nodules and buried in *barrancos*. And along the coast, quiet and secluded little bays unravel.

Take the motorway (TF5, 🚗) towards Santa Cruz. To avoid starting the day in a nightmare of traffic, keep on the motorway *past* La Laguna, then take the exit for Tegueste (TF13). Follow signposting for Las Canteras. Just past Las Canteras, at the junction, go right for Cruz del Carmen. Beyond the well-settled plain, you join the TF12, immersing yourselves in the coolness of the laurel forest and passing the Mirador Cruz del Carmen (📷✕*i*).

A kilometre further on, turn right for **Pico del Inglés**★ (40km 📷**P**26), your first stop. This fabulous *mirador*, where Walk 26 begins, has far-reaching views. Head back to the main road (TF12) and turn right. Restaurante Casa Carlos, 1km further on, is the landmark where Walk 25 starts and Walk 24 ends. Solitary houses speckle the ridges segmenting the isolated Afur Valley. Some 3km

Almáciga, perched above the coast (Car tour 2, Walk 28)

The Anaga Peninsula, from Casa Carlos (Car tours 2 and 4, Walks 24 and 25)

along, turn left to **Roque Negro** (TF136), a small village overshadowed by an enormous black basalt rock (48km 📷). The village square serves as a good look-out point: Afur can be seen far below in the shadows of these high crests (photograph page 119) and a wild beach, the Playa del Tamadite, lies beyond the village. I highly recommend a 4km detour to Afur (**P**25), just to experience the friendly bar and to stretch your legs with a walk to the picnic spot. The main tour returns from Roque Negro to the TF12 and heads left, after 3km passing a forestry house (56km 🏠📷) where Short walk 27-2 begins

At the 59km-mark, turn off left for **El Bailadero**★ (📷✕), where Walk 28 begins. From here on the road is flanked by dense laurel forest. Some 5km further on come to the lovely **Anaga Forestry Park** (**P**28a) — a better place to start Walk 28, if friends will play chauffeur. At the **Mirador de las Chamucadas** (65km 📷), you'll have good views down over Igueste, a seaside village built across the mouth of a *barranco* (visited later in the tour). The starting point for Short walk 30 lies 3km further on, when you reach a road striking off right. You could stretch your legs here by descending to the deserted hamlet of Las Casillas (**P**30), from where there is another fine view down to Igueste.

Descending in S-bends into open rocky terrain, pass a turn-off to Las Bodegas (69km), sheltered in a narrow *barranco*, half a kilometre downhill. La Cumbrilla is the village perched high on the ridge under which the road passes. **Chamorga** (**P**29), the most isolated village on Tenerife, lies at the end of the road, a couple of kilometres

23

further on. A loose smattering of white dwellings, the hamlet snuggles into the sides of a *barranco,* shaded by palms and loquat trees. Walk 29, only accessible by car, begins and ends here. (If you're an experienced hiker, then try *Alternative* walk 29 — a must!)

From Chamorga return to the Taganana turn-off (left, just below El Bailadero). Some 2km further down, turn left again (⌒). After passing through a tunnel under the Bailadero *mirador,* you overlook a landscape of razor-sharp ridges cutting down to the sea. **Taganana** (91km ✚▲ ✕⊕*P*27), where Walk 27 begins and Short walk 25-2 ends, is a brilliant array of white houses spread across the tumbling lower crests of the valley. Palms and colourful gardens make this settlement extremely photogenic. Roque de las Animas (the Ghosts' Rock) towers straight above the road 1km beyond the village. **Roque de las Bodegas** (93km ✕), with its roadside restaurant, is a busy tourist stop. Past **Almáciga**, **Benijo** (96km ✕*P*28b) is just a few cottages and a beach. But Restaurante El Frontón, with good food and magnificent views, is a pleasant place to take a break. From here the road continues to isolated El Draguillo (Short walk 28).

Retracing your route through the tunnel, follow the TF12 down the Barranco de San Andrés to the south coast. At **San Andrés** (115km ▲✕🚌), turn left for Igueste. The palms of Las Teresitas (Tenerife's only golden-sand beach) add a touch of the tropics, and the unofficial naturist beach of Las Gaviotas is glimpsed far below, at the foot of cliffs. Picturesque **Igueste** (123km ✕*P*30; Walk 30) sits at the end of this cliff-hugging coastal road.

From Igueste follow the coast all the way to Santa Cruz, then pick up the motorway (🚌) back to **Puerto** (174km).

Taganana, from the Mirador El Bailadero

3 SPECTACULAR NORTHWEST SETTINGS

Puerto de la Cruz • San Juan de la Rambla • Icod de los Vinos • Garachico • Punta de Teno • Teno Alto • Santiago del Teide • Icod el Alto • Puerto de la Cruz

153km/95mi; 6-7h driving; Exit A from Puerto (plan pages 8-9)

En route: ⊞ Barranco de Ruiz, Los Silos, Buenavista, road to Teno Alto, Santiago del Teide, around La Guancha, near the Mirador de Garachico; Picnics (see **P** symbol and pages 10-16): (15, 16), 17-20; Walks 14-21

*Except for the TF320, the roads are narrow and winding. Some people may find the road between Masca and Santiago vertiginous. The sign on the road to Punta de Teno is confusing, but the road is **not closed**; it is **dangerous in bad weather**, and you drive it at your own risk!*

A backdrop embroidered in greens highlights the small and picturesque villages, precipitous sunken valleys, superb coastal settings and sheer shadowy peaks that characterise the landscapes visited on this circuit.

Head west from Puerto on the motorway. When it ends, continue on the TF320. This coastal road passes below cliffs towering up to the left, while breakers crash below on the right (10km ⬛⯊ Mirador de San Pedro; 13km ⊞ Barranco de Ruiz). **San Juan de la Rambla** (16km ✕⯊) is a charming, fresh-white village overlooking the sea. Las Aguas, a neighbouring village with a swimming pool on the rocky shoreline below, is a picture-postcard scene glimpsed just before San Juan. All the way from Puerto to the northwestern tip of the island, you're immersed in banana palms and bright seasonal blooms.

Continuing along the TF320, come into **Icod de los Vinos★** (26km ✝🛏🏔⛰✕⯊⊕), on the fertile vine-growing slopes below El Teide. The 16th/17th-century San Marcos Church merits a visit. Just below the lovely church square is Icod's famous ancient dragon tree ... and the 'Butterfly House', a newer tourist attraction. Nearby Playa de San Marcos, a resort that never took off, is a small sandy beach surrounded by dark jagged cliffs (a 5km return detour).

Manorial homes amidst banana plantations come into view as you leave Icod on the TF42, hugging the coast. Come into **Garachico★** (32km ✝🛏🏔⛰✕⯊⊕M). This beautifully-situated village, once an important port, was destroyed by a volcanic eruption in the early 18th century. But a few buildings of interest survive: the 16th-century San Miguel Castle, the Baroque palace of the Marqués de Adeje, the 17th-century Convent of San Francisco, and the Church of Santa Ana (founded in 1548). Garachico is otherwise known for its inviting natural rock pools. The Roque de Garachico, rising up off the shore, bears a cross to protect the little town from another catastrophe. The town has undergone a restoration programme, so it's well worth wandering through.

Continuing west on the TF42, you skirt **Los Silos** (38km ✛🏪🍴) on a by-pass road. Walks 16 and 21 would take you into the impressive deep ravines that open out onto this village. Further along this fertile coastal plain lies **Buenavista** (42km ✕🏪⊕🍴), where Walk 20 ends. The village is walled in by high sharp crags, and gorges and valleys cut back into this cataclysm of rocks. Just past the Plaza de San Sebastián, where there is a small chapel on the right, turn off left, following signs for Punta de Teno. Five kilometres along the TF445, there are especially fine views from the **Punta del Fraile** (📷), where the island falls away into an indigo sea. The road continues to wind its way around and under rough indented cliffs, high above the sea, and then descends to the lighthouse on the dark volcanic promontory of **Punta de Teno** (52km 📷P20). This is one of the richest botanical areas in the Canaries. Swimming off the rocks in the crystal clear water here is a must! Revived, return to Buenavista (61km): at the junction, turn right on the TF436 for El Palmar.

El Palmar's lush curving valley lies well hidden above the coastal plain. A steep climb through rocky terrain covered in prickly pear, *vinagrera*, *verode*, *tabaiba* and wild geraniums leads you up past magnificently-terraced slopes. Walk 17 ends at **El Palmar** (67km). A kilometre further on, watch out on the right for a narrow country lane signposted to Teno Alto and follow it. (This turn-off is the starting point for Walk 20.) A steep climb (69km 🍴) takes you up to **Teno Alto** (75km ✕📷) — a tiny outpost of farms scattered across a tableland eaten away by

The mountains of Teno, with El Palmar in the valley (Car tour 3, near Walk 17)

enormous valleys. Scrub and pastures share the slopes. Alternative Walk 18, and Walks 19 and 20 pass through Teno Alto. Lunchtime? Try the simple home cooking in the bar/restaurant here, especially the *cabrito* (kid) and *garbanzos* (chickpeas) … and don't miss the wine. But if you're picnicking, and it's not too windy, then try the picnic spot a kilometre uphill (*P*19b): take the steep narrow road that climbs to the right of the village shop/ bodega. The road ends at another hamlet, La Siete. Use notes on page 14 to reach one of the best spots on the island (photograph page 99 and map pages 100-101). On your return through Teno, you might like to note that there is good wine and cheese on sale in the shop/bodega.

Return to the El Palmar road and head right. At the highest point on the road, park at the pass of **La Tabaiba** (89km ☞*P*19a) — to take in the dramatic difference between the El Palmar and Masca valleys — the former smooth and sweeping, the latter sharp and turbulent. Walk 19 begins here, and Alternative walk 18 crosses here en route to Teno Alto.

Winding down into deep gorges, a series of lay-bys and *miradors* allow you to pull over to appreciate the magnificient scenery, with especially mouth-watering views over charming **Masca** (94km ✗☞), a favourite village amongst the islanders themselves. (Masca is another popular walking base, and its *barranco* is explored in *Landscapes of Southern Tenerife and La Gomera*.)

Climbing out of the gorges, you cross a pass with spectacular views of El Teide; behind you, La Gomera, La Palma, and — if you're lucky — El Hierro can be see on the horizon. **Santiago del Teide** (100km ✚✗▣⊕Ħ) rests in a shallow valley just below. Here you join the TF82 and head north towards Icod de los Vinos. A great change takes place as you leave Santiago's treeless valley and enter the herbaceous greenery that envelops **Erjos** (*P*17), where Walk 17 begins. The pass of **Puerto de Erjos** (103km, ☞*P*18a, 18b) separates the two basins. One kilometre below the pass sits the friendly Restaurante

Fleytas — with great home cooking and pastries; it's the perfect afternoon tea stop. Walk 18 begins at the restaurant, and Short walk 18 ends here.

The unkempt countryside soon gives way to cultivated plots of vegetables and fruit trees. The Camel Centre is passed just above **El Tanque** (112km ✗♟), a long strung-out village. A turn-off left in the village would take you to the Mirador del Lomo Molino (1km west; ▣✗), with expansive views all along the northern slopes as far as Tacoronte. A couple of kilometres below El Tanque lies the **Mirador de Garachico** (▣✗ and nearby ⛁), from where you have the best outlook over the village setting and the offshore rock.

Superb views accompany the descent through hillside villages to Icod. Approaching the town, head right, first passing through **Icod**, then picking up the TF342 signposted to La Guancha. Barely 3km through Icod, the route takes you right, onto the TF342. The road climbs through rocky farmland to **La Guancha** (125km ✗♟⊕ and nearby ⛁; *P*15), where Walk 15 ends. Troughs full of scarlet geraniums brighten up the streets. From here head straight along the TF342 to another farming area set on steep slopes, **Icod el Alto** (136km ▣✗♟), where Walks 14 and 15 begin. The Mirador La Corona is 3km up a side road to the right as you enter Icod el Alto, but the Mirador El Lance (▣✗), built into the escarpment just past the village, is more convenient and offers the same far-reaching views. (Besides … La Corona's shrine can't compete with El Lance's well-hung Guanche statue.)

Rounding the escarpment and leaving the village, the road, cut into the sheer rock face, affords tremendous views on the descent into the Orotava Valley. *Carefully* follow the complicated one-way stystem through **Los Realejos** (✗♟⊕ and oldest ♱ on Tenerife). Just beyond Los Realejos Bajo, pick up the motorway heading east; then leave at Exit 36 (the Las Arenas exit) to head back east into **Puerto** (153km).

The lighthouse at Punta de Teno (Car tour 3, Walk 20)

4 QUIET CORNERS OF THE ANAGA

Puerto de la Cruz • Tacoronte • Bajamar • Punta del
Hidalgo • Batán • Las Carboneras • Taborno • Pico del
Inglés • La Laguna • Puerto de la Cruz

140km/87mi; 6h driving; Exit B from Puerto (plan pages 8-9)

En route: Picnics (see **P** symbol and pages 10-16): 22, 23a-b, (23c), 24,
26; Walks 22-27

This can be an afternoon's drive, but it's better to spend a leisurely day
over it: driving will be slow on the narrow winding roads. Hint: beyond
Punta del Hidalgo, refer to the large-scale map of the Anaga on the
reverse of the touring map.

D rive down to the coast and take a dip in the sea-water
pools (there are several choices), continue up to the
summits of the Anaga and wend your way down into
silent *barrancos* with dramatically-sited villages. Go for a
stroll in the laurel forest, then perhaps finish the day on a
cultural note: saunter around the streets of La Laguna.

Take the motorway (TF5) from Puerto as far as the turn-
off for El Sauzal. Pass under the motorway, then go right
immediately on the TF152 for **Tacoronte** (18km ✝▲▲✗
🚻⊕). The wooden statue of Christ in the 17th-century
church here is attributed with numerous miracles and is
revered by many of the islanders. Immediately past the
plaza, turn left on the TF16 and follow it all the way to
Tejina (28km ✗🚻), where a one-way traffic system
operates. At an unsigned T-junction, go left. At the large
roundabout outside Tejina, follow signs for Bajamar.
Colourfully-blooming bushes and creepers, together with
large banana plantations, enliven the landscape along
here. The village's tidal pools make the small-scale resort
of **Bajamar★** (32km ▲▲▲✗🚻⊕) a popular swimming
spot. A backdrop of severe rocky ridges and ravines over-
shadows the settlement, and an abundance of xerophytic
plants cling to the dark, abrupt inclines.

Continue on the same road to **Punta del Hidalgo★**
(35km ▲▲▲△✗🍴🚻**P**23a). It lies along a slight bay with
a rocky beach, across from Bajamar. The road ends past
the village, at a turning circle where high craggy crests
fall into the sea. Walks 22 and 23 set out from here.

Return to the roundabout outside Tejina and follow
signs to La Laguna. Follow the same signposting through
Tegueste (46km ✗🚻). **Las Canteras** (51km ✗🚻) straddles
a crest. At the highest point in the village, turn sharp left
(blind corner) onto the TF12, heading up into the magnificent laurel forest. A *mirador* (📷) on the right, 4km from
Las Canteras, affords captivating views of the lush green
undulating hills outside La Laguna. One kilometre above

Roque de Taborno (Picnic 24 and Walk 24)

the *mirador,* fork left for 'Batanes', to make for the isolated village of Batán, hidden in a valley deep in the spine of the peninsula. Keep right all the way downhill. Some 8km of winding road brings you down to **Batán** (*P*22), superbly sited in stunning mountain scenery. Having come all this way, why not walk to the picnic spot; you'll be amazed at the sheer hillside terraces and the paths that reach them. Walk 22 climbs this valley.

Back on the TF12, keep left for **Cruz del Carmen** (74km ✕ 📷*i*), a well-designed viewpoint, framed by the forest. From here you overlook the Aguere Valley of La Laguna and have more views of the ever-present Teide.

For a brief time you leave the dense forest, as you drive down to two more beautifully-situated villages — Las Carboneras and Taborno: 1km past the turn-off to Pico del Inglés, go left. At a fork, keep left (TF145) for Las Carboneras (downhill to the right lies Casa Carlos, where Walk 24 ends and Walk 25 begins). Valleys open up as you descend, and Punta del Hidalgo reveals itself for a moment. Roque de Taborno, shown above, is a prominent landmark sitting high atop the opposite ridge. At a further fork, again keep left. **Las Carboneras★** (85km ✕*P*23b) sits glued to a hill, encircled by cultivation. Walks 23 and 27 end here; Walk 24 starts out here. Chinamada (Walk 23, *P*23c), a tiny village of cave dwellings, is a further 2.5km along, should you wish to visit it (photograph page 112).

Now return to the fork passed earlier (TF138) and turn left. After descending a forested ridge, you come into **Taborno★** (90km 📷*P*24), where small dwellings are dispersed along the crest of the ridge, rising high above two deep *barrancos.* Walks 24 and 27 both pass through the hamlet, shown on page 126.

Return the same way to the main road and turn right. Then head left to **Pico del Inglés★** (99km 📷*P*26). Perched on the spine of this range that divides the island north and south, the *mirador* offers views down into the hidden cultivation of the Afur Valley, captures snippets of the coast, and looks out towards the island's guardian, El Teide. Walk 26 descends from here to Santa Cruz. From Pico del Inglés make for the charming university town of **La Laguna**, before returning to **Puerto** (140km).

5 THE SUN-BAKED SOUTH

Puerto de la Cruz • La Laguna • La Esperanza • El Portillo • Güimar • Arico • Candelaria • Puerto de la Cruz

224km/140mi; 6h driving; Exit B from Puerto (plan pages 8-9)

En route: ⊼ at Las Raices, Monte Los Frailes; Picnics (see **P** symbol and pages 10-16): 7, 8a, 13b; Walks 7, 8, 9, 13

Generally good driving, except for 30km of bumpy, narrow road along the TF28. The motorways are always busy. Part of the TF24 (between La Esperanza and the Arafo turn-off) is often enshrouded in low-lying mists. Note that there are no petrol stations en route between La Esperanza and Arafo — more than 68km.

From the greenest to the driest, from the lowest to the highest, and from forested to naked — this drive has it all. The higher inclines along the southern flanks of the island, missed by most tourists, are a dramatic contrast to the rich green slopes of the north.

Leave Puerto by Exit B and zip along the motorway (🚑) to La Laguna, where this tour *really* starts. Turn off for Las Cañadas 28km along, then take the second right, the TF24. Lush green pasturelands lie along the way to **La Esperanza** (34km ✕🚑), as you ascend the spine of the island. Beyond La Esperanza, keep right at the two junctions you encounter. Eucalyptus and pines forest the crest. From this vantage point, you have a number of *miradors* to enjoy. The *zona recreativa* Las Raices is passed on the left (39km ⊼) just before you reach the first *mirador,* **Pico de las Flores** (40km 📷), overlooking the luxuriant slopes down to Santa Cruz and up to the Anaga range. Next is **Mirador Ortuño** (📷), with views to the pine-robed slopes of El Teide. Pass the Arafo turn-off soon after: you'll be returning to this road later in the tour. A detour of 1km is required to reach the Mirador de Cumbres (📷), which also looks out over the northern slopes.

La Crucita (60km 📷**P**7) is the point where pilgrims cross the TF24 on their way from the north to Candelaria. Walk 7 follows this ancient route. As you near the pass at the top of the road, the pines subside and rocky protrusions, covered in *retama,* take over the landscape. Later the terrain changes again, as rich volcanic tones — maroons, purples, russets, wines, greys and blacks — flow in and out of each other. A couple of kilometres further on, a section of the roadside embankment attracts your attention with its grey and white horizontal stripes. Pass the turn-off for the Observatorio de Izaña (69km): it can be visited on Fridays from 10am-2pm, but only by appointment (tel: 922-605 200).

El Portillo (75km ✕wc**P**8a, 13b) is the starting point for Walks 8, 9 and 13. Here turn round and head back along the TF24 for 20km, to the Arafo turn-off passed earlier in the tour. You now descend to the southern slopes. Pines accompany you partway on this descent but, as you approach the lower slopes (⊼ at Monte Los Fraíles), loose scatterings of chestnuts take over. The Güimar basin opens up ahead, revealing corners with great ravines cutting back deep into the steep escarpment. High brown stone terraces step the slopes of this productive agricultural centre. Vineyards, interplanted with vegetables, cover the greater part of the land. Bypass the centre of Arafo (where Walk 7 ends) and continue straight on through **Güimar★** (116km ⛰✕🚪⊕M). Keep to the left of the church here, then turn right along the *avenida*. At the T-junction turn right, to rejoin the TF28 for Fasnia.

This bumpy old road winds in and out of shallow ravines before climbing out of the basin along the eastern escarpment, from where you have a superb view over the valley and towards the Anaga Peninsula. From here on, the monotone landscape becomes more harsh. Trees have vanished, save for the fine-branched Jerusalem thorn bordering the roadside. In April and November, its yellow blossoms cheer up this countryside. Rock walls terrace the slopes. You'll notice, too, masses of roadside caves — squared, arched, and with doors or gates. Often the doorways open into enormous chambers.

Fasnia (133km 🚪⊕) is a pleasant country village set back off the road. Between here and Arico there are few settlements, and the land looks almost abandoned. The restaurant uphill from the petrol station at **Arico** (147km ✕🚪⊕) makes a good lunch stop. Turn left here on the TF625, down to the motorway (TF1 🚪), then head left for Santa Cruz. After 24km turn off to **Candelaria★** (179km ✝⛰✕🚪⊕). The basilica (1958) houses the new statue of Nuestra Señora de la Candelaria, the island's patron saint. (The original statue was supposedly found in 1390 by Guanche herdsmen and was lost in a tidal wave in 1826.) The large square on the seafront near the modern church (photograph pages 6-7) is quite impressive, with red-rock statues representing Tenerife's ten former Guanche chiefs. From here follow the motorways to **Puerto** (224km); 12km from Candelaria, be sure to take the 'Autopista del Norte' connection, to bypass Santa Cruz.

☀ Walking ─────────

This book covers most of the best walking on Tenerife — enough ground to keep even the most energetic hiker going for a good month. While all the best walks in the popular Orotava Valley have been included, don't miss the Teno and Anaga peninsulas.

I hope you will also use this book, together with the bus timetables on pages 136-140, to make up your own walk combinations. I've indicated where routes link up on the walking maps, and the fold-out touring map shows the general location of all the walks. One word of caution: **Never try to get from one walk to another on uncharted terrain!** Only link up walks by following paths described in these notes or by using roads or tracks. Do not try to cross rough country (which might prove dangerous) or private land (where you might not have right of way).

There are walks in the book for everyone.

Beginners: Start on the walks graded 'easy', and be sure to look at all the short and alternative walks — some are easy versions of the long hikes. You need look no further than the picnic suggestions on pages 11 to 16 to find a large selection of *very* easy rambles.

Experienced walkers: If you are used to rough terrain and have a head for heights, you should be able to tackle

El Draguillo (Walk 28)

all the walks in the book, *except those recommended* **for adventurous walkers only**. Of course, you must take into account the season and weather conditions. For example, in rainy weather some of the *barranco* walks will be unsuitable; in strong winds or snow do not plan excursions to the mountains! And, always remember that **storm damage can make these routes unsafe at any time!** Remember, too: always follow the route as described in this book. If you have not reached one of the landmarks after a reasonable time, you must go back to the last 'sure' point and start again.

Experts: Provided that you are used to sheer, unprotected drops and scree, *and provided that conditions are still as described in the notes,* you should be able to tackle all the walks in the book.

G uides, waymarking, maps

Guides are easily found on Tenerife: ask at a tourist information office. **Waymarking** and **signposting** have always been quite good on Tenerife, but as this edition goes to press, plans are afoot to bring path recognition up to 'Euro' standards (as has already happened on some of the other Canary Islands). This will take a couple of years and, unfortunately, no official guidance is yet available. There will be three types of waymarking:

- *Red and white* waymarks indicating GR routes ('Grandes Recorridos': long-distance footpaths);
- *Yellow and white* waymarks indicating PR routes ('Pequeños Recorridos': short trails of up to six hours);
- *Green and white* waymarks indicating SL routes ('Senderos Locales': local trails, up to about 10km long).
- For all these routes, right-angled stripes indicate a 'change of direction; an 'X' means 'wrong way'.

Once the work is finished, the authorities will publish a trail map, and we will add the trail numbers to our maps.

The **maps** in this book, based on fairly old military maps, have been very greatly adapted using notes made on the ground and reproduced at a scale of 1:50,000. There are several good maps covering the whole island available for walkers at bookshops and kiosks.

D ogs — and other nuisances

Dogs, in general, aren't a problem. However, you will encounter some ferocious ones — hopefully chained or in enclosures. I mention where I encountered troublesome dogs. Village dogs are usually small and noisy, but the sight of a stick sends them scurrying. However, if you do a lot of walking on the island, you are bound to meet at least one unfriendly monster, rightly guarding his territory. You may wish to invest in a 'Dog Dazer', an ultrasonic device which frightens dogs off without harming them. These are available direct from the Sunflower Books web site: www.sunflowerbooks.co.uk. My greatest problem is abandoned dogs; they always recognised me as a 'softy' and latch onto me.

Hunters may startle you with bursts of gunfire, but they present no other worries. They come out in force on the weekends and on holidays — always trailed by yapping dogs. The hunting season lasts from August through December.

Give chained **billy goats** a wide berth; they don't like intruders! Other than that, you've no other pests to worry you on Tenerife — there are no poisonous snakes or insects.

What to take

If you're already on Tenerife when you find this book, and you haven't any special equipment such as a rucksack or walking boots, you can still so some of the walks — or buy yourself some equipment at one of the sports shops. *Don't* attempt the more difficult walks without the proper gear. For each walk in the book, the *minimum year-round equipment* is listed. Where walking boots are required, there is no substitute: you will need to rely on the grip and ankle support they provide, as well as their waterproof qualities. All other walks should be done with stout lace-up shoes with thick rubber soles, to grip on wet, slippery surfaces.

You may find the following checklist useful:

walking boots (which *must* be broken-in and comfortable)
waterproof rain gear (outside summer months)
long-sleeved shirt (sun protection)
first-aid kit, including bandages, plasters and antiseptic cream
plastic plates, cups, etc
windproof
spare bootlaces
sunhat, sunglasses, suncream
whistle, compass, torch

up-to-date bus timetables (see page 7)
plastic bottle with water purifying tablets
long trousers, tight at the ankles
knives and openers
fleece
extra pair of socks
plastic groundsheet
small rucksack
insect repellent
Dog Dazer (see under 'Dogs')

Please bear in mind that I've not done *every* walk in this book under *all* weather conditions; use your judgement to modify the list according to the season.

Walkers' checklist

The following points cannot be stressed too often:

- **At any time a walk may become unsafe due to storm damage or bulldozing**. If the route is not as described in this book, and your way ahead is not secure, do not attempt to go on.
- **Walks for experts only** may be unsuitable in winter, and all mountain walks may be hazardous then.
- **Never walk alone** — four is the best walking group. If someone is injured, two can go for help, and there will be no need for panic in an emergency.
- **Do not overestimate your energies**: your speed will be determined by the slowest walker in the group.
- **Bus** connections at the end of a walk may be vital.
- **Proper shoes or boots** are a necessity.
- **Mists** can suddenly appear on the higher elevations.
- **Warm clothing** is needed in the mountains; even in summer take some along, in case you are delayed.
- **First-aid kit, compass, whistle, torch** weigh little, but might save your life.
- **Extra rations** must be taken on long walks.
- **Always take a sunhat with you**, and in summer a cover-up for your arms and legs as well.
- Read and re-read the important note on page 2, the country code on page 39, and the guidelines on grade and equipment for each walk you plan.

Where to stay

For walkers **Puerto de la Cruz** is the best base. Attractive Puerto has an efficient bus service and a wide choice of accommodation. Most of the walks described are easily accessible from here; the remainder require a few bus changes (making for long days, but little inconvenience). However, recognising that **the south** has become the major tourist centre, the bus timetables include some important connections from the Playas. Consider spending one or two nights in the solitary and peaceful **Parador de las Cañadas**. You can book in advance: Parador Nacional de las Cañadas del Teide, Santa Cruz, Tenerife; telephone: 922/38 64 15. If you're adventurous, you could also stay at the refuge on El Teide: see page 66. Finally, if you're not tied into 'package' accommodation, there are hotels in La Laguna and Santa Cruz, bringing you closer to the Anaga walks. For Teno, try the hotels in Garachico and San Marcos, near Icod de los Vinos. See the three web sites suggested on page 6!

Weather hints

Island weather is often unpredictable, but there are a few signs and weather patterns that may help you forecast a walking day.

Tenerife is blessed with year-round walking weather. The north, unfortunately, has more than its fair share of rain, but pleasant temperatures. The south soaks up the sun. Wind strikes the southern coastline east of Los Cristianos, but rain is a rarity.

Weather patterns are influenced by two **winds**: the northeasterly trade winds (the *alisio*) and the easterly or southeasterly wind from the Sahara (the *tiempo del sur*). Two other winds blow very infrequently: a northwesterly wind from the north Atlantic and a southwesterly wind from the tropics. Both carry heavy rains and storms. In winter this usually means snow in the mountains. Only the 'westerlies' carry clouds that blanket Las Cañadas. Luckily these winds are very rare.

The northeasterly trade wind, the *alisio,* which prevails for much of the year, is easily identified by low-lying fluffy clouds — which add so much character to your island photographs. These clouds hover over the north for much of the year. They sit between 600-1500m/2000-5000ft and, above these heights, clear blue skies prevail. The Las Cañadas area, however, is the only beneficiary of these beautifully clear days.

The *tiempo del sur,* quite different, brings heat and dust. The temperature rises considerably, and the atmosphere is filled with very fine dust particles. This weather is more frequent in winter than in summer. It seldom lasts more than three or four days. These days are always good for walking (but in summer stay under tree cover!); even if it's a little warm, the sky is cloudless, although a bit hazy.

The only wind that could really spoil your day is the one from the tropics. It *always* brings heavy rains which cover the whole island. This wind is recognisable from its uniform cloud cover. Fortunately it rarely blows.

The winds bring fresh breezes off the sea, making the days very pleasant for walking. And remember, the clouds don't block out the sun altogether; especially on the heights, you will tan (or burn) due to the combination of sun and wind. Don't forget a sunhat! On the other hand, when walking at the higher altitudes, one must always be prepared for the *worst* as well: all seasons can be experienced in one day!

Spanish for walkers

In the countryside, a few words of Spanish can be useful, to greet people and to ask directions.

Here's an almost foolproof way to communicate in Spanish. First, memorise the few short key questions and their possible answers, given below. Then always ask the many questions you can concoct from them **in such a way that you get a 'sí' (yes) or 'no' answer.** *Never* ask an open-ended question such as 'Where is the main road?' Instead, ask the question and then *suggest the most likely answer yourself.* For instance: 'Good day, sir. Please — where is the path to Afur? *Is it straight ahead?'* Now, unless you get a *'sí'* response, try: *'Is it to the left?'* If you go through the list of answers to your own question, you will eventually get a *'sí'* response —probably with a vigorous nod of the head — and this is more reassuring than relying solely on sign language.

Following are the two most likely situations in which you may have to practice some Spanish. The dots (...) show where you will fill in the name of your destination. Approximate pronunciation of place names is given in the Index, starting on page 141.

- **Asking the way**

  The key questions

English	Spanish	pronounced as
Good day,	Buenos días,	Boo-**eh**-nos **dee**-ahs
sir (madam, miss).	señor (señora, señorita).	sen-**yor** (sen-**yo**-rah, sen-yo-**ree**-tah).
Please —	Por favor —	**Poor** fah-**voor** —
where is	dónde está	**dohn**-day es-**tah**
the road to ...?	la carretera a ...?	la cah-reh-**tay**-rah ah ...?
the path to ...?	la senda de ...?	lah **sen**-dah day ...?
the way to ...?	el camino a ...?	el cah-**mee**-noh ah ...?
the bus stop?	la parada?	lah par-**rah**-dah?
Many thanks.	Muchas gracias.	**Moo**-chas **gra**-thee-as.

  Possible answers

is it here?	está aquí?	es-**tah** ah-**kee**?
straight ahead?	todo recto?	**toh**-doh **rec**-toh?
behind?	detrás?	day-**tras**?
to the right?	a la derecha?	ah lah day-**ray**-cha?
to the left?	a la izquierda?	ah lah eeth-kee-**air**-dah?
above?/below?	arriba?/abajo?	ah-**ree**-bah?/ah-**bah**-hoh?

- **Asking a taxi driver to return for you**

English	Spanish	pronounced as
Please	Por favor	**Poor** fah-**voor**
take us to ...	llévanos a ...	l-**yay**-vah-nos ah ...
and return	y volver	ee vol-**vair**
for us at ...	para nosotros a ...	**pah**-rah nos-**oh**-tros ah ...

(Point out the time when you wish him to return on your watch.)

A country code for walkers and motorists

The experienced rambler is used to following a 'country code' on his walks, but the tourist out for a lark may unwittingly cause damage, harm animals, and even endanger his own life. A code for behaviour is especially important on Tenerife, where the rugged terrain can lead to dangerous mistakes.

- **Only light fires** at picnic areas with fireplaces. Stub out cigarettes with care.
- **Do not frighten animals.** The goats and sheep you may encounter on your walks are not tame. By making loud noises or trying to touch or photograph them, you may cause them to run in fear and be hurt.
- **Walk quietly** through all hamlets and villages, and take care not to provoke the dogs.
- **Leave all gates just as you found them**, whether they are at farms or on the mountainside. Although you may not see any animals, the gates have a purpose: they are used to keep goats or sheep in (or out of) an area. Here again, animals could be endangered by careless behaviour.
- **Protect all wild and cultivated plants.** Don't try to pick wild flowers or uproot saplings. Leave them for other walkers to enjoy. Obviously fruit and other crops are someone's private property and should not be touched.
- **Never walk over cultivated land.**
- **Take all your litter away with you.**
- **DO NOT TAKE RISKS**! This is the most important point of all. Do *not* attempt walks beyond your capacity, and do not wander off the paths described if there is any sign of mist or if it is late in the day. **Do not walk alone**, and *always* tell a responsible person *exactly* where you are going and what time you plan to return. Remember, if you become lost or injure yourself, it may be a long time before you are found. On any but a very short walk near villages, be sure to take a first-aid kit,

Taginaste rojo (Echium wildpretii)

Above: Greenovia aurea

Below: cardón (Euphorbia canariensis)

whistle, torch, extra water and warm clothing — as well as some high-energy food, like chocolate.

Organisation of the walks

The 30 main walks in this book are grouped in four general areas: the Orotava Valley, Las Cañadas, the northwest (including the Teno Peninsula), and the Anaga Peninsula. I hope that the book is set out so that you can plan your walks easily — depending on how far you want to go, your abilities and equipment, and the season.

You might begin by looking at the large fold-out map inside the back cover. Here you can see at a glance the overall terrain, the road network, and the location of all the walks. Quickly flipping through the book, you'll see that there is at least one photograph for every walk, to give you an idea of the landscape.

Having selected one or two potential excursions from the map and the photographs, turn to the relevant walk. At the top of the page you'll find planning information: distance/time, grade, equipment, and how to get there by bus. If the grade and equipment specifications are beyond your scope, don't despair! *There's almost always a short or alternative version of a walk,* and in most cases these are far less demanding of agility and equipment.

When you are on your walk, you will find that the text begins with an introduction to the overall landscape and then quickly turns to a detailed description of the route itself. The large-scale maps (see notes on page 34) have been annotated to show key landmarks. Times are given for reaching certain points in the walk, based on an average walking rate of 4km/h, with extra time allowed for ascents and steep descents. *Do compare your own times with those in the book on a short walk, before you set off on a long hike.* Remember that I've included only *short stops* at viewpoints; allow ample time for photography, picnicking and swimming.

These symbols are used on the walking maps:

▬▬▬	main road	824	height (m)	⁑	danger! vertigo!
▬▬	secondary road	♂	*galería*, tap, spring	⚐/†	church/shrine
▬▬	minor road or lane	⋜	pylon, wires	⊹	cemetery
▬▬	track	⊖	car parking	▪	specific building
- - - -	path or steps	🚐	bus stop	�	picnic tables
12→	main walk	A	*choza*	∩	cave
6→	alternative	P	picnic (pages 10-16)	👓	best views
▬▬	watercourse *(canal)*	◺	rock formation	📖	map continuation

1 PUERTO DE LA CRUZ • PLAYA DEL BOLLULLO • CAFE VISTA PARAISO

See also town plan pages 8-9   **Distance:** 7km/4.3mi; 3h

Grade: The coastal stretch is easy; however the climb to the café and bus stop (just under 350m/1150ft) is strenuous, with loose stones underfoot initially. Some vertiginous stretches of path along the coast, some of which can be avoided (but see also Alternative walk 1).

Equipment: stout walking shoes (boots preferable), light fleece, sunhat, suncream, rain-/windproof, picnic, water

How to get there: The walk starts in Puerto de la Cruz.
To return: 🚌 101 from the TF217 at Cuesta de la Villa (not in the timetables, but runs approximately half-hourly)

Alternative walks

1 Puerto de la Cruz — Playa del Bollullo — Café Vista Paraíso: 7km/4.3mi; 3h; easy; access and equipment as main walk. *If you wish to avoid the vertiginous stretches on the main walk,* you can return from the viewpoint over Playa del Bollullo to the El Rincón lane and follow it past El Rincón (Restaurante San Diego), picking up the main walk again at the 1h25min-point. Timings are about the same.

2 Puerto de la Cruz — Playa del Bollullo — Puerto de la Cruz: 7.5km/4.6mi; 2h15min; grade, access and equipment as main walk. *This version avoids the steep climb to Café Vista Paraíso.* Follow the main walk to the 1h25min-point, where you reach a narrow road just after climbing out of a *barranco*. Turn right and follow the road (keeping straight ahead past a restaurant a couple of minutes along) for about 15 minutes — until you see your outgoing path below you in the *barranco*. Descend into the *barranco* and return to Puerto on your outgoing route.

Right on your doorstep, this excellent 'starter walk', with magnificent seascapes of towering cliffs, couldn't be more convenient. And if vertigo is a problem, or the climb to Café Vista Paraíso looks too daunting, then opt for one of the alternative walks.

Referring to the town plan on pages 8-9, **start out** at **Plaza Viera y Clavijo**, at the top end of Avenida Aguilar y Quesada. Follow Calzada Martiánez over the bridge to the shopping centre, and then turn left immediately into Camino las Cabras. Steps take you up to Camino de San Amaro, where you again turn left. This pretty promenade is also stepped. Not far uphill, veer left to the **Mirador de la Paz**, from where you have a superb view over Puerto.

From here descend to the **Camino de la Costa**, a walkway built into the face of the cliffs, with a striking outlook all along the coast. After five minutes, it takes you up to a street (Leopoldo Cólogan) just beside the HOTEL SEMIRAMIS (**30min**). Turn left and, when the street swings right, keep straight on, now on a tarmac lane (still the Camino de la Costa). Passing below the last apartment block on the right, and a CAR PARK, the way takes you under the main Carretera del Este, and a neatly-paved road

comes underfoot. You look up at verdant slopes sliding off into the sea and disappear amidst banana plantations. When the road ends, dip down into the little **Barranco de la Arena**, filled with stong-scented lavender, *tabaiba*, marguerites, and sticky-leafed *lengua de gato*. Out of the ravine you meet another lane (**55min**), where a right turn leads to El Rincón; keep left. *(Alternative walk 1 returns to this point and follows the lane to El Rincón.)* At the next junction, turn left again. Soon you're heading along the cliff-top above **Bollullo Beach** — a pretty spot.

Just past the BOLLULLO RESTAURANT (closed Wed; **1h**), leave the lane and turn off on a path that heads along the cliff-tops, scattering lizards galore. Minutes along, you pass the path down to Bollullo Beach. Head right, behind a banana plantation, on a path hemmed by a stone wall and tamarisk trees. *(But Alternative walk 1 turns back, to follow the El Rincón lane.)* Soon steps disappear down the face of the escarpment: this sometimes-vertiginous path leads to the naturist beach you can see up ahead — also popular with surfers. Ignore it and continue ahead, along a vertiginous stretch of path with sheer drops to the left and no side-railings. Most people pop through the

wall into the banana plantation, and pop back out a couple of minutes along, where the path *does* have a railing. The view along these sea-cliffs is spectacular. Soon another stairway disappears below, part of it collapsed. Here the path swings inland, and you ascend an overgrown *barranco*. A flight of steps take you up a precipitous escarpment — another slightly vertiginous stretch, and unavoidable.

Ten minutes up, you leave the *barranco* and join the narrow ROAD TO EL RINCON (**1h25min**): turn left. *(But for Alternative walk 2, turn right.)* At a junction a couple of minutes along, keep left on a concrete lane. Some 100m/ yds after passing a balconied house the lane ends, and your way becomes a private track, closed to vehicles. Your ascent route to Café Vista Paraíso leaves to the right here, marked with red and yellow arrows. For the present, ignore it, and continue ahead on the track. Enormous clumps of *cardón* are splashed across the cliffs ahead; behind you, to the left, is the spread of Puerto; sheer terraced hillsides, bare of cultivation, rise above you.

When you spot a large tree at the side of the track and a small building off to the right, descend the path to the left just before them. Dropping down through terracing, you suddenly find yourselves at the edge of the cliffs, above a narrow beach. Head right, down to FINCA ANCON (**2h**), set in splendid isolation on a high promontory — a perfect picnic spot, with spectacular sea views.

Returning to the ascent point for Café Vista Paraíso takes about 10 minutes. Now *carefully* follow the way-

marks steeply uphill; initially the path is quite skiddy, with loose stones underfoot. The zig-zags afford fine views of the lower Oratava Valley. Some 35 minutes uphill, steps bring you up onto a road, where you turn left. Here live the *crème de la crème* — all behind high walls. CAFÉ VISTA PARAISO (**2h50min**) lies a couple of minutes along (open from 12 noon; closed Mondays). Enjoy the spectacular views!

Then climb the steps to the right just past the café and turn left on the road at the top. Turn right over the TF5 and, at the junction that follows, head right uphill, to **Cuesta de la Villa** (**3h**). The bus stop is on the right, where you meet the TF217.

View down over Playa del Bollullo

2 AGUAMANSA • BENIJOS • TF21

Map pages 54-55
Distance: 7.5km/4.6mi; 2h
Grade: easy; descent of 300m/1000ft.
Equipment: stout shoes, sunhat, fleece, rain-/windproof, picnic, water
How to get there: 🚐 345 from Puerto to Aguamansa (Timetable 2); journey time 45min; *alight at the third stop after the 'Aguamansa' road sign.* 🚗: park below the km15 road marker.
To return: 🚐 345 (Timetable 2) from the TF21 — to Puerto (journey time 40min), or back to your car at Aguamansa. Alternatively, take 🚐 347 (Timetable 10) from Benijos to La Orotava
Alternative walk: Aguamansa — Chanajiga — Palo Blanco: 12.5km/7.8mi; 4h15min; moder-

ate climb of 100m/330ft and descent of 600m/1950ft; access and equipment as above. Return as Walk 14, page 80. Follow the main walk to the *choza* at the 1h06min-point. Take in the view, then return to the junction, a minute back uphill, and continue along this track all the way to Chanajiga. Ignore the many turn-offs. Landmarks or cairns along the way include Lomo de los Tomillos (1h40min); Salto Bangarro (1h 53min); Lomo Alto (2h15min); (Choza Cruz de Luis) 2h40min. On reaching the tarred road, continue past it to the car park and Chanajiga picnic area (3h). To continue to Palo Blanco, an hour away, pick up Walk 14 at the 2h45min-point (page 82).

This walk is a good starter — it should whet your appetite. The combination of greenery, flowering heather, and the bucolic charm of the highest farmland in the Orotava Valley makes this a pleasant afternoon's stroll.

Start out where you leave the bus at **Aguamansa**. Walk uphill past the KM15 ROAD MARKER (where you could park), and then turn right on the narrow tarred road SIGNPOSTED 'LAS FUENTES 1000 M', ascending past the fenced trout farm. If you would like to visit the trout farm (open 10am to 3pm), where you can also see injured and rescued birds of prey, you can get in via the back entrance, which you pass just four minutes up this road. Some 100m/yds beyond this entrance, just before a gate, climb the path up to the left, keeping right at a fork. This path runs parallel with the road, now above to your left.

Ten minutes uphill, turn right on a forestry track (PISTA DE BENIJOS). Ignore the track joining from the right half a minute along. Weather permitting, the volcanic cone of El Teide will be in full view, peeping over the western wall of the Orotava Valley. From this vantage point, however, it's difficult to believe that this is Spain's highest mountain (3718m/12,195ft)!

Just over 1km along, fork right on a track to **Galería La Fortuita (30min)**, one of the island's many water sources.

From these *galerías* (tunnels), water is piped to all parts of the island. The water is tapped from underground 'reservoirs', where there is a continuous supply of water resulting from condensation (the Canary pine plays a particularly important role: see notes on page 50). Tenerife relies very heavily on these water sources, because there are no natural wells and few streams with a permanent flow of water.

After returning to the main track, ignore the fork to the right within the next 20 minutes. A little over 10 minutes later, you enter a narrow gulley and cross an overgrown old stone bridge above a dry river bed with huge boulders. Within two minutes you pass **Galería Pino Soler (1h)**; the two-storey GREEN BUILDING now houses the old railway engines. Five minutes later, at a junction, turn right down-hill. *(But if you are doing the Alternative walk, keep straight on.)*

A minute downhill, take the first track branching off right (**1h06min**). (There used to be a magnificently sited *choza* just before this turn-off, but it was missing in 2007; we hope it will be replaced, and have left the symbol on the map.) Just before reaching a junction, ignore a track off to the right. Turn right at the junction, soon passing a farm track off to the left. A LONE PINE TREE, two minutes further on, is your next landmark. Keep right here, ignoring a footpath off to the left. But a couple of minutes later, just after crossing a COVERED WATER CHANNEL, descend to the left on a faint track. The track ends in a ravine with some interesting basalt rock formations. You climb out of the ravine on a path at the left of a narrow cultivated plot, to cross a beautiful section of hillside stepped in lush and colourful fields ... and to enjoy more views.

Keeping straight on along the terracing, in minutes you join a CONCRETE LANE (**1h35min**). In the setting shown op-posite, a steep descent follows, as you look straight over the impressive Orotava Valley. Around 10 minutes later you meet the TF326 east of **Benijos**: bus 347 stops here, at the foot of the lane. Heading on to the TF21, turn right along the TF326. On the first bend, take a concreted short-cut on the right, initially passing a small SHRINE. Then continue along the road to the right. The TF21 is a further 10 minutes away. The stop for buses heading north to Puerto is on the opposite side of the road, outside the CAFÉ (**2h**; usually closed between 1pm-4pm). But if you're returning to Aguamansa, catch the bus on the near side of the road.

3 AGUAMANSA • LA CALDERA • CHOZA CHIMOCHE • LOMO DE LOS BREZOS • AGUAMANSA

Map pages 54-55

Distance: 7km/4.3mi; 2h30min

Grade: easy-moderate climb/descent of 400m/1300ft; the descent from Lomo de los Brezos is steep and slippery.

Equipment: stout shoes, sunhat, fleece, rain-/windproof, picnic, water

How to get there and return: 🚌 345 from Puerto (Timetable 2; journey time 45min) or 🚗 to/from the Aguamansa trout farm (main entrance)

Short walk: Aguamansa — La Caldera — Aguamansa: 3km/2mi; 1h; easy. Follow the main walk to the crater, circle it, and return the same way.

Here's a short walk with plenty of variety — patches of forest, ravines, high and naked escarpments, shady moss-green paths, and some good views.

Start out at the TROUT FARM. From the main entrance, cross the road and walk uphill to the bus shelter. Follow the wide earthen path that heads up into the pines and heather directly behind the bus shelter (SIGNPOSTED 'CAMINO DE LAS PIEDRAS'). Ignore a branch-off to the right a few minutes uphill. Five minutes up, cross over a forestry track; then ignore another small path to the right a few minutes later. When you come to a fairly wide GRAVEL TRACK (**25min**), turn right. Behind you is the impressive mountain range enclosing the eastern side of the Orotava Valley. On reaching the tarred road that circles **La Caldera**, bear right; through the trees, you will see the crater (*la caldera*) below you on the left. There's a pleasant bar/restaurant ahead (closed Wed) and beyond it a large parking area and bus stop.

Continue by circling the crater on the road. Ignore a first gravel track off to the right, but go right immediately after it on the next track (SIGNPOSTED 'ZONA DE ACAMPADA'). (*But for the Short walk remain on the tarred road here.*) Follow this track through slender pines. About 45 minutes uphill (SIGNPOST: 'POSADA DE LAS BESTIAS'), a wide earthen trail (your return route) strikes off to the left. Turn sharp right, on the main track. A small gorge lies below. Beyond an enormous gravel deposit, you pass **Galería Chimoche**, a very important water source (see notes pages 44-45). Behind the two buildings, hidden in the rocky-faced embankment, is the *galería* ('water gallery' or tunnel). **Choza Chimoche** (**1h40min**; Picnic 3) sits in a sheltered hollow further up the track. Continue up the track at the left of the shelter for a few minutes, to an even lovelier picnic spot by the mouth of a ravine, the **Barranco de Los Llanos**.

46

Los Organos and (inset) Choza Chimoche

From the ravine retrace your steps for 20 minutes and head back to more garden-like surroundings. Turn off right at the T-junction below Galería Chimoche. The track to the left is the route you climbed from La Caldera; you now head right on a wide earthen trail which skirts the ravine below. Five minutes from the turn-off you come to a small flat area called **Lomo de los Brezos (2h10min)**. (The track ends just around the bend.)

From Lomo de los Brezos descend to the left on a path marked by a cairn. This path is called the '**Camino de las Crucitas'**, named for the three little wooden crosses that stand on the left near the bottom of the path. From this serene spot, a forestry track is visible below on the right: it goes to Choza El Topo and Choza Almadi (Walk 5). You soon cross it — going straight ahead 30m/yds, to a tree bearing TWO YELLOW CIRCLES. Now follow the path behind the tree, shaded by tall heather, leafy trees, and the occasional pine. The trees are bearded with moss and lichen (photograph page 52).

Having crossed the track to **Galería La Puente**, your path rejoins the same track, which you follow to the left. A few minutes along, pass a track forking off to the right. Just beyond it, you'll see your return path, also on the right: it's the path you ascended from Aguamansa. Two minutes downhill the path collides with a magnificent old pine that must be about 5m/15ft in circumference at the base of its trunk. Ignoring all the narrow side-paths, in five minutes you reach the MAIN ROAD AND BUS STOP (**2h30min**).

4 AGUAMANSA • PINOLERIS • LA FLORIDA

Map pages 54-55
Distance: 4.5km/2.8mi; 1h15min
Grade: moderate descent of 550m/1800ft. *All on tar, but a very popular walk.*
Equipment: stout shoes, sunhat, fleece, rain-/windproof, picnic, water
How to get there: 🚌 as Walk 2, page 44
To return: 🚌 373 from La Florida to La Orotava (not in the timetables; hourly departures at

45min past); journey time 10min; *change to* 🚌 350 (Timetable 3); journey time 30min
Alternative walk: Aguamansa — Choza Chimoche — La Florida: 13km/8mi; 3h25min. Moderate climb of 400m/1300ft and steepish (at times) descent of 900m/2950ft; access as Walk 3; equipment and return as above.
Do Walk 3 before this walk.
Photo: shrine at the 20min-poin

Here's a perfect rural setting of peaceful farmlands. Bright-blooming flower beds enliven country cottages, wild fields are grazed under the watchful eyes of shepherds, ageing chestnuts stand guard over the declining slopes, and neat stone walls hide the season's produce.

Start out where you leave the bus at **Aguamansa**. Walk uphill past the KM15 ROAD MARKER and then turn left, steeply downhill, on a lane beside a bus shelter (just a few metres/yards below a bar/restaurant). After 200m/yds take the second right turn (CAMINO DE MAMIO). From here on you follow a country road. Colour and greenery flow out of the landscape all the way. Hedges of white-flowering chimney broom *(escobón)* border the fields. Beyond a reservoir over to the left and a lane to the right, keep left at a JUNCTION (**20min**). Some 250m/yds further on, by the well-cared-for SHRINE shown above, a road comes in on the right (from Choza Perez Ventoso; Short walk 5). Keep straight on (left) here, ignoring a road to the right almost immediately. Five minutes later, *don't miss your turn off.* It comes up just past houses 12 and 11b: turn right on a lane by house 68.

The road curves back sharply left and descends to a T-JUNCTION (**45min**). Turn left here, passing a rural life museum with traditional stone and thatched buildings. At the next junction, by a church on the left, turn right downhill (sign: 'LA FLORIDA, PINOLERIS'). Keeping to the main lane, continue down through **Pinoleris**. A good five minutes later, at a T-junction in **La Florida Alta** (**1h**), turn left, ignoring a fork to the left immediately after. At the main junction beyond the SCHOOL in **La Florida**, turn left on the road (which *may* be signposted 'LA OROTAVA'). The STOP FOR BUS 373 is on your right (**1h15min**). Or continue steeply uphill for 15 minutes to the TF21 and turn right to a nearby BUS STOP (frequent buses to Puerto).

5 LA CALDERA • CHOZA EL TOPO • CHOZA ALMADI • PINO ALTO • LA FLORIDA

Map pages 54-55

Distance: 20km/12.5mi; 5h30min

Grade: a fairly strenuous full day's walk. It's easy, almost level walking to Choza El Topo, then a strenuous climb of 350m/1150ft to Choza Almadi, followed by a steep descent of 1000m/3300ft. *This hike is only suitable in good weather.* There are only three shelters between La Caldera and Pino Alto, and temperatures can drop very suddenly on these heights (1200m/4000ft and above).

Equipment: walking boots, sunhat, warm fleece, rain-/windproof, whistle, picnic, water

How to get there: 🚌 345 from Puerto to La Caldera (Timetable 2); journey time 50min
To return: 🚌 373 from La Florida to La Orotava (not in the timetables; departs hourly at 45min past the hour); journey time 10min; *change to* 🚌 350 (Timetable 3); journey time 30min

Short walk: La Caldera — Choza El Topo — Choza Perez Ventoso — Aguamansa: 6km/3.7mi; 1h45min. Easy, level walking to Choza El Topo, then a steep descent of 200m/650ft to Choza Perez Ventoso (slippery when wet); access/return on 🚌 345 (Timetable 2); stout shoes or walking boots, sunhat, fleece, picnic, water. Follow the main walk for 1h, then descend the steep trail behind Choza El Topo. When you come to a wide track (with a *choza* above on the right), keep downhill. Asphalt soon comes underfoot, and the remains of ruined Choza Perez Ventoso are on your left. Walk down to a junction with a shrine on your left and turn left. Keep along this road until you meet a T-junction in Aguamansa, where you climb up left to the bus stop on the TF21.

This walk requires a little energy, as you head up into cloud territory at about 1450m/4750ft. But wherever you pull up to rest, a panorama will unfold around you — if you beat the morning clouds. For most of the way, your views sweep along the whole Orotava Valley, from El Teide down to the ocean, and over to the western tip of the island. Grand specimens of indigenous pines will capture your attention. Out of cloud territory, you'll descend through terrraced plots shaded by chestnut trees, a rural scene little changed by tourism. This is where I like to ponder, in the shade of a chestnut, and soak up the superb coastal view that lies before me.

The walk starts at the BAR (closed Wed) at **La Caldera**. Leaving the bus, walk past the bar and then fork left on the gravel forestry track signposted 'PISTA MONTE DEL PINO' (it *may* also be signposted to Los Organos). This track through heather and pines is easy to follow. Not far along, you cross a bridge straddling the end of a narrow ravine.

About **10-15min** along various SIGNS appear; follow the main track around to the left. (Walks 6 and 7 head south at this point.) In the sweeping U-shaped curve of the track, you'll notice a pine-covered slope. These tall and gracious trees look almost ornamental, with long wisps of pale green lichen hanging from their branches (see photograph page 52). There are more such corners further on. The highest farms in the valley, nestled in against the walls of the escarpment, lie a little below the track. The fields up here are not cultivated and seem to have reverted to grass. Groves of chestnuts are loosely scattered below the route. Lower down, orchards can be seen through the pines. You pass a large stone building, built into the embankment (**35min**) and, five minutes later, ignore a cairn-marked turn-off to the left, which *may* be signposted to Aguamansa. (Walk 6 descends that track.)

Choza El Topo (Picnic 5) is reached under **1h** from La Caldera. A table and bench await the tired and hungry. This shelter is another good viewing spot for the Orotava Valley. Keep straight on beyond this shelter *(but for the Short walk, descend the track behind the* choza*)*. Within the next 20 minutes, after crossing the **Barranco del Infierno**, the real ascent begins. Carved into the mountainside, the track now zigzags lazily up towards Choza Almadi. It's a steady climb. There's a possibility that you'll be swallowed up by clouds or mist as you approach the summit of the track, at 1450m/4750ft. The way curves back into an inner valley in the range, and then begins to descend out into the Orotava Valley again, with good views of the Los Organos mass of dissected rock. A little further along, the coastline unrolls.

Notice the dampness in the air. On cloudy days, all the plants are saturated with dew, giving rise to an interesting phenomenon: the majestic Canary pine plays a very important ecological role. The prevailing northerly winds carry clouds to the northern slopes, and create an atmosphere which causes condensation. The drippings from this moisture were measured over the period of a year and yield an incredible 2000 litres per square metre! This may not mean much to you — until I tell you that a reasonable rainfall for a year gives about 500 litres per square metre. This is the reason for the continuous planting of trees in bare or denuded areas of the forest: to feed the underground reservoirs described on pages 44-45.

As you approach Choza Almadi, varying shades of browns from the ploughed plots far below and greens from sprouting plants catch your attention. You come to an intersection, where **Choza Almadi** (**2h50min**) sits below the track. Take a break here, before beginning the

View to El Teide from the Orotava Valley

descent. Then turn left immediately and head straight downhill below the shelter. This descent is so steep that you'll find yourself almost leaning backwards! Some grand old trees tower overhead. At a fork two minutes downhill, you can take either branch (they rejoin); the upper fork to the left has better views. Now ignore all the many turn-offs to the right. Keep left all the way down to **Cruz de las Lajitas (3h 15min)**. There is a small white shrine to the left, buried in flowers, and a *choza*. The view over the Orotava Valley is superb.

A second clearing is reached just a little further on: take the earthen track to the left, going straight downhill. Five minutes downhill, when this track forks, go right.* Beyond a stretch of deep shade, at a T-junction, go right (even though Pino Alto may be signposted to the left here.) Quickly coming to another T-junction, turn left on a wider track. Now the gradient eases, and it's a fairly easy descent to a four-way junction, aptly called **Cuatro Caminos**. Turn left here on a track signposted 'LA OROTAVA, PINO ALTO, SANTA URSULA'. Ignore a track off left (which *may* be signposted to La Orotava) and continue

*The sure-footed among you might like to use the map to take a more direct route to Pino Alto, but be warned: the route is very steep and slippery, with deep ruts (the track is used at weekends by locals with motorcycles, quad bikes, etc). The short-cut paths — where they still exist — are waymarked with faded yellow dots. *Don't attempt this route in wet conditions under any circumstances!*

ahead. The track bends round to the right and passes a small *choza* (**4h10min**). From here the track descends in long zigzags (ignore all turn-offs to the left and a narrow asphalt road to the right) until it finally tarmac comes underfoot and you reach a T-junction with a narrow asphalt lane.

Turn left and follow this lane towards Pino Alto. Watch for a track off left (the difficult route mentioned in the footnote on page 51) and a shrine beside the road. Two minutes later, on the right (just beyond a house with a tall lone palm tree in its garden), you can opt for a three-minute short-cut — or remain on the road to descend to Pino Alto.

Pino Alto appears, perched high above the rest of the valley. This typical Canarian village has a superb outlook. The church, with its grand balconied plaza, is an ideal place to get your breath back and absorb the view. Just beyond the church, turn left at a T-junction. The escarpment wall rises up protectively behind the village and, below, vineyards (which produce a white wine) cover most of the land.

Following a steep descent and then a slight climb, you reach a junction (**5h30min**) which marks the beginning of **La Florida**. The STOP FOR BUS 373 is just downhill to the right (the road *may* be signposted to LA OROTAVA). Other-

wise continue steeply uphill for 15 minutes to the TF21 and turn right to a nearby BUS STOP (from where you can catch one of the frequent buses to Puerto).

Lichen-festooned pines between Choza El Topo and Choza Almadi — a setting typical of many island walks.

6 LA CALDERA • LOMO DE LOS BREZOS • AGUAMANSA

Map pages 54-55; see also photograph page 47

Distance: 12km/7.5mi; 4h20min

Grade: strenuous climb of 400m/1300ft and descent of 500m/1650ft. You must be sure footed and have a head for heights. At time of writing the exposed stretches were securely protected, but at any time railings can always be broken by rock falls.

Equipment: stout shoes or walking boots, sunhat, warm fleece, rain-/windproof, picnic, water

How to get there: 🚌 345 from Puerto to La Caldera (Timetable 2); journey time 50min, or 🚗

To return: 🚌 345 from Aguamansa — to Puerto (Timetable 2; journey time 45min), or back to your car at La Caldera

Shorter walk: La Caldera — spectacular chasm — La Caldera: 9km/5.6mi; 3h10min. Access, grade, equipment as above. Follow the main walk for 1h45min, then return the same way for 🚌 345 or your car.

Have you ever wondered what lies *above* Los Organos? This classic walk takes you up into cloud-catching peaks. Between these fractured pinnacles lie chasms of exuberant vegetation.

The walk starts at the BAR (closed Wed) at **La Caldera** (Picnic 6a). Leaving the bus, walk past the bar and then fork left on the gravel forestry track signposted 'PISTA MONTE DEL PINO' (it *may* also be signposted to Los Organos, the rock formation shown on page 47). About **10min** along, various SIGNS appear: follow 'CHIMOCHE' and 'CAMINO A CANDELARIA', by taking the wide earthen path that strikes right off the track here (Walk 5 continues along the track.) The three little crosses you pass give this path its name: **Camino de las Crucitas**.

Pink-flowering Cistus *flanks the route between Lomo de los Brezos and the Los Organos turn-off.*

Fifteen minutes further uphill you come to a small flat area, **Lomo de los Brezos**. Now cross a track and follow the path slightly to the left, up the hillside. The way divides here and there, braiding itself up the slope. The side-on view of Los Organos and the eastern escarpment is quite impressive. It's hard to believe that the route winds up into those walls! At just over **40min** up, a path branches off right; keep left. A few minutes later, turn left at an IMPORTANT JUNCTION (**45min**). *(Walk 7 turns right here, to make for La Crucita.)* Beyond the junction your path *descends* at first; just 1m/yd along, two trees (one either side) have had part of their bark hacked away just above eye-level, and there is also a spot of blue paint on a rock on the right of the path some 50m/yds from the junction. Not far around the slope, you'll notice hundreds of the small rosette plants shown on page 39 (*Greenovia aurea*) on the rock face. Grey-green velvet-leafed bushes (*Sideritis* or 'Canarian edelweiss') will also catch your eye.

You leave the Chimoche side of the slope and begin the long climb above Los Organos. You pass a viewpoint at a rocky promontory and soon enter a plunging gorge, surrounded by precipitous, sharp peaks. Although the path is *very* exposed in places, sturdy railings allay feelings of vertigo, and you can enjoy the primeval setting.

At about **1h45min** you reach the END OF THE GORGE. *(The Shorter walk turns back here.)* Some minutes further on there is a fine view of Aguamansa's trout farm — pro-

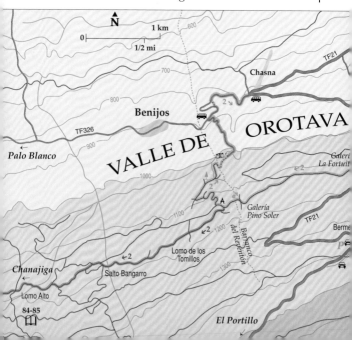

vided the clouds aren't too low. Beyond this viewpoint the path progresses eastwards, zigzagging up and down across what seems inaccessible terrain. You swing into the enormous **Barranco de la Madre**, deep in the escarpment.

On leaving this valley and entering a wood, you soon find yourselves at *the highest point in the route* and must ***watch carefully*** for your turn-off on the left: it is currently marked with GREEN ARROWS on the ground and a GREEN-PAINTED 'II' carved in the trunk of an adjacent tree. This path heads down towards a large rocky 'hump' but, be-

Taginaste
(Echium
decaisnei)

Cerrajón (Son-
chus ortunoi)

Palo sangre
(Sonchus
tectifolius)

Retama
(Spartocytisus
supranubius)

Peorera
(Andryala
cheiranthifolia)

fore reaching it, you descend a 'ramp' of rocks on the left side of the hump. Once off the ramp, your continuation becomes clear.

On joining a track coming from the right (**3h**), keep left. Some 35 minutes downhill, turn right at a T-junction. Rounding a bend, turn left immediately, down a path marked by a small pile of stones. A fairyland descent through woodland follows, on a path carpeted with pine needles. The bushes and trees are thickly-bearded with wispy lichen. A ravine runs alongside you on the left.

Ten minutes downhill you cross straight over the La Caldera/Choza Almadi forestry track (Walk 5), on a cairn-marked track (which *may* be signposted to Aguamansa). A steep descent takes you down to farmlands. You pass a track off right, then a path off left. You head into a beautiful unkempt countryside of fields, large chestnut trees and and white-flowering *escobón*. A track joins from the right, and you head down a concrete lane bordered by crumbled stone walls. On coming to a junction, keep left. Entering **Aguamansa**, go left again, for the short stiff climb up to the BUS SHELTER on the TF21 (**4h 20min**). Rooftops weighed down with vividly-coloured hanging plants and roadside planters brimming with flowers are your last memories of this walk.

Senecio sp.

Codeso (Adeno-
carpus foliolosus)

Margarita
(Argyranthemum)

Valo
(Plocama
pendula)

Sea fennel
(Crithmum
latifolium)

7 THE CANDELARIA TRAIL: LA CALDERA • LA CRUCITA • ARAFO

Use the map on pages 54-55 as far as Montaña de las Arenas and the map on page 58 from Montaña de las Arenas to Arafo. See also photograph page 11

Distance: 12.5km/7.8mi; 5h

Grade: very strenuous, with a steep climb (800m/2600ft) and steep gravelly descent (1500m/4950ft).

Equipment: walking boots, sunhat, warm fleece, rain-/windproof, long trousers, whistle, picnic, water

How to get there: 🚌 345 from Puerto to La Caldera (Timetable 2); journey time 50min
To return: 🚌 121 from Arafo to Santa Cruz (not in the timetables): departs Arafo at 45min past the hour until 20.45 (hourly Mon-Fri; every *second* hour Sat, Sun, holidays); journey time 50min; *change to* 🚌 102 to Puerto (Timetable 1); journey time 1h

Short walk: La Caldera — Choza Chimoche — La Caldera: 5.5km/ 3.5mi; 1h45min. Moderate climb/descent of 300m/1000ft; equipment as above, but stout shoes will suffice. Referring to the map, follow *Walk 6* (page 53) to the major junction met at 45min. Keep right here. Just uphill from the junction, below the large pine, bear right on a path. The path ends at the Barranco de los Llanos (55min); follow the forestry track downhill a couple of minutes, to Choza Chimoche. Descend the track behind the shelter, picking up Walk 8 at the 4h15min-point (page 63).

This hike follows an old pilgrims' way known as the Candelaria Trail. It originally began at La Orotava. It climbs the steep escarpment of the central massif and then twists endlessly down to the sea at Candelaria. Today, the land between Arafo and Candelaria is so built up that the few pilgrims who still make the journey leave the trail at our destination, Arafo. The Virgin of Candelaria is Tenerife's patron saint, whose Assumption is celebrated each year on August 14-15th. This long, but gratifying walk offers superb panoramas, encompassing corners of immense beauty.

Start out by following WALK 6 (page 53) up to the important junction (**45min**), where Walk 6 heads left: here turn *right*. Barely a minute up, the main path veers off round the right-hand side of the ridge. You do *not*! At this point you are just below a large pine: continue up the ridge, to the left of the pine. *(The path to the right leads to Chimoche and is the Short walk route.)* For the first few minutes of the climb, you are in a sunken path. A couple of minutes up, ignore a path branching off to the left. The route will eventually take you up and over the *cumbre*.

As the climb steepens, more of the valley becomes visible through the sparse pine growth. Some 25 minutes from the last turn-off, on a bend, you look over into a strip of bare *barranco* that emanates a soft mixture of pinks,

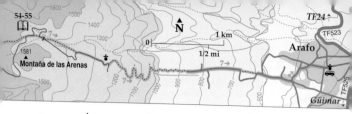

54-55

TF24 ↑
TF523

1581
Montaña de las Arenas

Arafo

TF525

Güímar

mauves, browns and greys. Seconds up, your path briefly runs alongside the thin, vertical wall of serrated rock shown opposite. The vegetation undergoes a change here: small bushes of Canarian edelweiss (*Sideritis*) turn white as their velvety leaves catch the sun, and scraggy chimney broom (*escobón*) and *retama* take control of the slope. The path is so colourful that it's easy to forget the wider landscapes on view.

All the way up, the vast view stretches across the upper inclines of the Orotava Valley, where more and more land is being given over to buildings. At **1h35min** you find yourselves sheltered between a low dyke and a few pines. A faded arrow points you through a gap in this natural rock wall. From here, you can see the path heading across the escarpment. Another patch of writing on rocks, and a WHITE ARROW pointing left, are your next landmarks. The path climbs steeply through rocks and over stones in a multi-coloured volcanic landscape. A good look-out point lies midway between the dyke and the TF24 above.

When you reach **La Crucita (2h20min**; Picnic 7) at an altitude of 1980m/6500ft, get out your anchor! From here on it's down, down, as you descend the southern escarpment. Cross the TF24 and, 50m/yds along to the left, turn right on a forestry track. The isolated valley you are about to enter lies far below. The entrance to the valley is blocked by an enormous naked black mound, Las Arenas. You have the stupendous view shown on page 11: dark, pine-sprinkled slopes drop down to a coastal plain tessellated in faded browns and greens. The sea stretches out into the distance.

Three minutes down the track, your path strikes off to the left and slithers its way down the stark slope. Large WOODEN PEGS stand on either side of the path. These will be your path waymarkers until you reach Las Arenas. The descent will be at a snail's pace: there's loose gravel under foot, and the slope looks almost vertical. Within minutes, you cross the track. Turn left: your continuation is 10m/yds downhill, on the right. Soon you head back into pines, under which *codéso* and broom shelter. The path forks just above the track. If you fork right, along the crest of the ridge, the stretch is vertiginous, but railings help part of the way. (An alternative is to fork left to the track, then turn right.) Where the main (crest) path rejoins the track by a CAIRN, continue downhill for 20m/yds, then take the path on the left, on a bend. It squiggles through the trees, past lovely picnic spots on relatively flat land and, at the edge of the wood, with spectacular views (another setting for Picnic 7). Where the path is faint, keep the shallow ravine on the left within sight, and you're sure to be okay. Sporadic small dots of red paint help you along.

Recross the track once more, and again find the path

At 1h the path runs alongside a thin vertical wall of rock.

slightly below and to the left. At the next track crossing, find the ongoing path again a few metres downhill and on the left. A minute downhill finds you in a shallow *barranco:* descend this for a couple of minutes and then swing out of the ravine and around the hillside.

Smooth black sand soon comes underfoot. The outline of a rounded volcanic hill completely disrupts the landscape as it appears through the trees. You come face-to-face with this bulging black monster, **Montaña de las Arenas**, at **3h15min**. It obliterates everything. The track is not far below; shortly, you rejoin it. Follow it downhill for about a minute; then, on the next bend, cut off right across the sand. On meeting the track again, leave it after two minutes (just past a metal gate): take the path that veers straight ahead off the track, and keep alongside the ravine. (The track heads slightly away from the ravine, to the right, at this point.) Gran Canaria is on the horizon. Arafo, your destination, is far below, and the immediate landscape reveals an intriguing beauty: chestnut trees are the sole survivors in these black sands. Bent and crippled, these 'triffid' creatures have never managed to raise their backs. It's a unique sight.

Some seven minutes later, when you next meet the track (on a bend), follow it downhill. In ten minutes you reach a simple STONE REFUGE that the pilgrims visit. To continue, head to the bend in the track just below the refuge and take the small path down to the left (cairn, white arrow, red dot), briefly encountering scrub and bushes.

Scrubland is eventually replaced by a Canary pine forest, and you pass some proud old specimens. The way (always marked with CAIRNS) splinters and rejoins. Ignore the faint path forking left: keep straight downhill. Shortly your route swings left across the hillside and, in a few minutes, you strike off right on a faint path (just opposite a CAIRN on the left), crossing an old *canal* a minute down. Five minutes below the *canal*, you come to the edge of the forest. Again you wind your way through scrub. A few minutes down, you encounter another small *canal*. Then your path meets a narrow TARRED LANE (**4h25min**).

From now on, head *straight down,* whether by path or track or road, to arrive at **Arafo**. Here you meet a narrow tarred road: turn right. Pass between the houses and turn left at the junction. Walk past a tiny bubbling fountain, benches, and flower troughs splashing out colour. Take the first right, then go right again. This brings you to the MAIN SQUARE (**5h**), where the bus stop is to the right.

8 EL PORTILLO • CORRAL DEL NIÑO • CHOZA CHIMOCHE • LA CALDERA

Distance: 17km/10.5mi; 5h

Grade: moderate but long, with an ascent of 250m/820ft at the start and a fairly steep descent of 1000m/3300ft

Equipment: walking boots, sunhat, warm fleece, rain-/windproof, picnic, water

How to get there: 🚐 348 from Puerto to El Portillo (Timetable 5); journey time 1h
To return: 🚐 345 from La Caldera to Puerto (Timetable 2); journey time 50min

Views to El Teide, just beyond Montaña del Limón

A rolling landscape of perfectly-rounded volcanic mounds, mellow, glistening slopes, and the occasional chirp of calling birds sets this walk apart from the others. Over an hour on an asphalt road does not sound like a very appealing beginning to a walk. But the TF24 is not a busy road, except on weekends. The striking natural beauty of the landscape, and the omnipresent El Teide, detract from the little traffic encountered.

Start out in front of the RESTAURANT at **El Portillo**: head east on the La Laguna road (TF24). **Montaña del Alto** will be your first significant landmark, on your left. You'll pass the small gravel track to its *choza* (Picnic 8a) in about **15min**. Along the roadside, the white and yellow blooms of *margarita del Teide*, *retama* and Canary flaxweed prove their worth in springtime. The road climbs some 250m/820ft to Corral del Niño. Being just outside the perimeter of the crater, it is not exactly like the landscape of Las Cañadas (Walk 9) — it lacks the aggressive sharpness. There's a smooth, flowing undulation here. As you progress, El Teide becomes complete behind you, and there are wide-ranging views of the Orotava Valley on cloudless days. The weird white buildings of the observatory on Izaña catch your attention.

In under **1h10min**, just before the 'Corral del Niño' SIGN, turn off left on a wide track. It takes you into a rolling sea of colours. The sun catches all the hidden tones as you follow the contours. You're crossing a giant palette, as you head down towards the pines far below. Pebble-sized scoria covers much of the land, and volcanic mounds rise like giant anthills.

An hour down the track brings you the ruins of **Choza J Ruiz de Izaña** (**2h10min**). From here take the well-defined path cutting a loop off the forestry track. Rejoining the track in two minutes, turn left. Barely one minute along (some 75m/yds), head right on your continuing path, hedged in by *retama*. **Montaña del Limón**, a small volcanic mound with burgundy-red slopes, soon comes into view on your right.

The forest begins rather shyly, with small scattered pines. The path zigzags symmetrically down to the track by a '**Cumbrita Fría**' sign (**2h50min**), where you turn right. You'll see plants with twigs like bottle-brushes, called

codéso (see drawing on page 56). During the winter, they're just a pleasing green, but in spring they enliven the landscape with their brilliant yellow blossoms. Some 20 minutes downhill, on a bend, you pass a fork off to the left and, around 10 minutes later, you leave the main track to turn off to the right for Choza Chimoche: a CAIRN waymarked '**Cuevitas de Limón**' marks the turn-off. (The main track continues left to the Ramón el Caminero picnic site and the TF21, an hour's walk away.)

The track now steepens considerably. You cross another forestry track at **Pasada del Fraile**. Not far above Choza Chimoche, the track ends, and a path brings you to the *choza*. If forestry work confuses the route, always keep right, near the beautiful ravine on your right.

Facing **Choza Chimoche (4h15min)**, your continuation to La Caldera is the second (descending) track to the right. (The first track to the right climbs to the Barranco de los Llanos.) You swing behind the shelter, dipping into a small flat area — a very picturesque spot for a picnic. After descending for a little over 10 minutes, the track passes **Galería Chimoche**. A few minutes later, you come to a T-JUNCTION and keep left downhill.

On coming to the tarred road which circles **La Caldera**, turn left for the car park and bus stop (**5h**). If you have time to spare before your bus leaves, head for the nearby bar/restaurant.

9 LAS CAÑADAS

See map pages 68-69; see photographs pages 19 and 67
Distance: 18km/11.2mi; 4h45min

Grade: easy ascent of 200m/650ft; short descent. But the walk is *long*, and there is only one bus a day; you must press on!

Equipment: stout shoes, long trousers *and* shorts, gloves, warm fleece, rain-/windproof, sunhat, picnic, water

How to get there and return: 🚌 348 (Timetable 5) from Puerto to El Portillo (journey time 1h) and back from the Parador de las Cañadas (journey time 2h)

Short walk: Montaña de Majuá — Piedras Amarillas — Parador de las Cañadas: 8.2km/5.1mi; 2h20min. Easy; equipment and access as above, but leave the bus at the turn-off for the El Teide cable car and return from the *parador*. From the cable car turn-off, continue south along the TF21 towards Montaña de Majuá, the large brown mound on the left-hand side of the road. Three minutes along, turn off on the track heading towards it. The national park management have done some waymarking here; it is one of their suggested routes (No 16). First climb to the top of Montaña de Majuá, then continue along the track. Ignore all turn-offs — *especially at areas near beehives, signed 'Peligro, Colmenas' (danger, bees).* An intriguing volcanic landscape unfolds. Some 55 minutes along the track, you come upon some little houses hidden in the rock. A good 10 minutes later, you pass through a barrier, soon meeting the Las Cañadas track followed in the main walk. Turn right along it and pick up the main walk at the 3h30min-point; the *parador* is 50min away.

Few people will ever walk on the moon, but this ramble inside Tenerife's great volcanic crater, Las Cañadas*, must be a close approximation of the weird and awesome lunar landscape. Tenerife has been a bed of volcanic activity for millennia. In fact, this activity is responsible for far more change on the island than are the elements. Controversy still exists about how the great crater of Las Cañadas was formed. One opinion claims that it is an enormous depression: Las Cañadas was originally covered by an dome. The collapse of the dome created the double crater which makes up this gigantic cauldron — the western side below the Roques de García and the eastern side stretching back to El Portillo. The other theory claims that erosion and the elements cut a large valley, opening to the north, and that this valley was later filled in by the surging up of El Teide and its off-sider, Chahorra. In either case, the crater was created some 300,000 years ago. The most recent activity here was a mere 200 years ago, when Chahorra (Pico Viejo) blew its top.

The following figures will give you some idea of the immensity of Las Cañadas: its diameter is almost 16km/ 10mi and its perimeter an astounding 45km/28mi. Much

---

*The *cañadas* are plains of sedimentary rock or gravel, but the name 'Las Cañadas' is commonly applied to the crater in which these plains lie (see overview photograph on page 67).

of it is surrounded by craggy, inconsistently-peaked walls, the highest point being Montaña de Guajara (Walk 12), 500m/1650ft above the floor of the crater, but all of 2717m/8905ft above sea level. El Teide is the majestic centrepiece.

Start at **El Portillo**'s BAR/RESTAURANT: walk up the road to the CAÑADAS VISITORS' CENTRE and take the gravel track across the road from the car park. The track quickly disappears into turbulent terrain and spilled masses of sharp rock. In **5min**, ignore a fork to the left and walk round a barrier (for vehicles). There are no turn-offs on this walk; you remain alongside the crater walls for nearly the whole hike. But at this point the walls on your left are rather insignificant, and it's not yet obvious that you're inside a crater. Smooth and perfectly-shaped scoria cones testify to former volcanic activity. The subtly-coloured *cañadas* give a touch of the desert. In winter these shallow gravelly plains often fill with water from melting snow.

As the track makes its way towards the escarpment, a perfectly-formed volcanic cone is seen ahead to the right: **Montaña Mostaza**. Further along, a beautiful tall wine-coloured rock formation appears in the wall itself. Some time later, you pass more interesting rock formations surrounded by beds of loose gravel; Japanese rock gardens come to mind. Then you descend to the **Cañada de las Pilas** (**2h**), a long gravel 'lake' with 'islands' of rock.

Half an hour later, having crossed a small crest, you look across the large expanse of the even more impressive **Cañada de la Grieta** (**2h30min**). Small crumbling animal pens sit in sheltered corners of the rock, a reminder of the days when the *cañadas* were grazed. A feeling of desolation hangs over the place, but in spring the *taginaste rojo*, the 'Pride of Tenerife' (see page 39), cheers the slopes on the left with its conical tower of close-knit red blooms.

The large flat-topped peak that has been shadowing you around the last few bends is **Guajara**, and you soon pass the turn-off left for the ascent. Ignore the TRACK off right (**3h45min**) to Montaña de Majuá and the Teide cable car. *(The Short walk comes in here.)* Next the bizarrely-sculpted **Piedras Amarillas** (Yellow Stones; photograph page 19) catch the eye; this is an unsurpassed viewing point for the western side of the crater. Beyond these rocks you join a tarred road and leave the park. Just beyond the park barrier, there is a stony short-cut path on the right. Plunge in and find your way. The **Parador de las Cañadas** (**4h45min**), has a café and its own visitors' centre (open daily from 09.15-16.00).

10 EL TEIDE

NB: You must have a (free) permit to climb El Teide. This can only be obtained *in person* from the offices of the Parque Nacional in Santa Cruz (4th Floor, Emilio Calsadilla 5; open 09.00-14.00 Mon-Fri except holidays). The building is southwest of '4' on the town plan on page 9, almost at the junction with Calle de la Marina. You must present your passport (or a photocopy) and stipulate a two-hour time slot for your arrival, so *allow plenty of time for the ascent — up to a good 6h!*

See map pages 68-69

Distance: 8km/5mi; 4h50min *for the ascent;* 16km/10mi; 7h45min *return.*

Grade: *very strenuous* ascent and descent of 1367m/4485ft; however, the path is good. *Take this walk very seriously: problems can include altitude sickness, no drinking water en route, and finding both the Refugio de Altavista and the cable car station at the summit closed.* The cable car *(teleférico)* may stop running *at any time* due to strong winds, in which case you'll have to descend on foot. Be prepared! Pay particular attention to the weather. Summer is obviously the best time for this hike (but be on the hill by dawn). In winter don't attempt it if there is *even the most remote chance of bad weather.* I describe the walk as a one-way ascent to the summit and return by cable car — harder on the lungs, but easier on the legs. The best way to tackle this hike, however, is to climb to the Refugio de Altavista and spend the night there. Early in the morning, make the final ascent to catch the sunrise, and descend on foot. The *refugio* is usually open all year round, but reservations are *essential:* see 'NB' above. (Once in a while the refuge *does* have to close — due to lack of water or other problems.)

Equipment: walking boots, warm fleece, windproof, sunhat, gloves, long trousers, thick socks, picnic, *plenty of water*

How to get there and return: 🚌 348 from Puerto to/from the Montaña Blanca turn-off (Timetable 5); journey time 1h35min, or 🚗: park at KM40 on the TF21. *The average walker will not complete the walk in time to travel both ways by bus. You will have to arrange for friends or a taxi to take you to the start of the walk or collect you at the end.*

Alternative walk: El Portillo — Montaña Blanca — El Portillo: 18.5km/ 11.5mi; 5h15min. Moderate-strenuous, with an ascent of 700m/2100ft; equipment as above, but walking shoes will suffice; access as Walk 13 and return on the same bus, or 🚗 to/from El Portillo. Follow *Walk 13* (page 77) to the 20min-point, where Walk 13 turns right. Turn *left* here and, at a junction three minutes later, keep right. From here on just refer to the map; the route to Montaña Blanca (2h40min) is straightforward. After leaving the summit, return down the track, then take the first track off left (about 20min down). Metres/yards along, strike off left on a path. This takes you back to your outgoing route within 30 minutes.

There are not many high volcanic mountains where one can begin the assault at well over halfway up, but we start this climb at the 2350 metre-mark. Another plus is that you needn't be a mountaineer to tackle this hike: from bottom to top, there's an easy-to-follow path. *But you must be **very** fit.* Among the problems you may encounter is altitude sickness — the signs usually being nausea and a headache. This often results when ascending too quickly. A slower ascent, with frequent rests, may relieve your sickness but, if it persists, it's best to turn back.

Take heed, too, of the warnings under 'Grade' above.

El Teide is the result of numerous volcanic eruptions. Chahorra, to the west of El Teide, was probably the most significant, and El Pilón (the peak itself) is still active. El Pilón rose over an older and much larger crater called La Rambleta, which lies just to the left of the cable car station near the summit.

Start out at the turn-off to Montaña Blanca at KM40. Follow the track towards Montaña Blanca. The ascent of El Teide is No 7 in the national park's scheme, so you will see small plaques with that number along the way. The landscape here — blanketed in pumice and scoria, inter-rupted by the occasional patch of jagged rock, wallows in desolation. Some **10min** from the bus stop ignore a track off right (the return route for the Alternative walk). In **20min** you pass two short-cut paths to the left. The *second* of these used to be my choice of route, but it may still be closed to walkers (again for conservation reasons). As you rise up, don't forget to look back at the unique view. In the Cañadas lie what look like rough mounds of chocolate. The walls clearly delineate the limits of the crater. The visitors' centre is but a few daubs of white.

In **35min** the route of the Alternative walk from El Portillo joins from the right, and eventually (**1h20min**) you come to an old car park (2750m/9000ft), just below the summit of **Montaña Blanca**. For those ascending El Teide, this is where the real climbing begins. A park

Las Cañadas from the summit of El Teide. Gran Canaria rises in the distance above a sea of clouds.

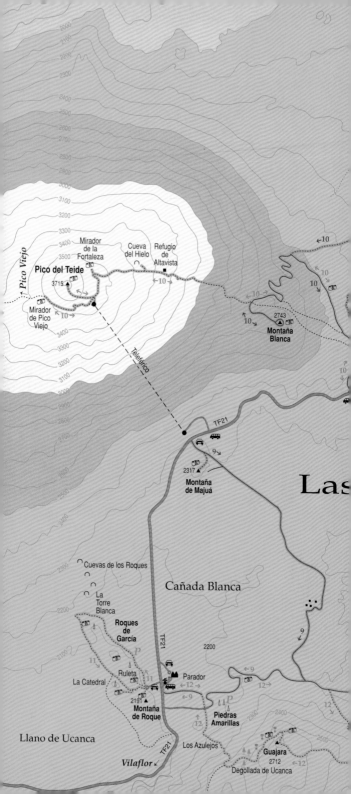

Mirador
de la
Fortaleza

Cueva
del Hielo

Refugio
de
Altavista

Pico del Teide

3715 ▲

←10→

Mirador
de Pico
Viejo

↑ Pico Viejo

←10→

2743
▲ Montaña
Blanca

←10→

Teleférico

TF21

9↘

2317 ▲
Montaña
de Majuá

Las

Cuevas de los Roques

Cañada Blanca

La
Torre
Blanca

Roques
de
García

2200

9↘

TF21

11↘

Ruleta

11↘

La Catedral

Parador

←12→

2191 ▲
Montaña
de Roque

←9→

12→

Piedras
Amarillas

12↓

Llano de Ucanca

Los Azulejos

Guajara

2712
Degollada de Ucanca

TF21

Vilaflor ↙

12→

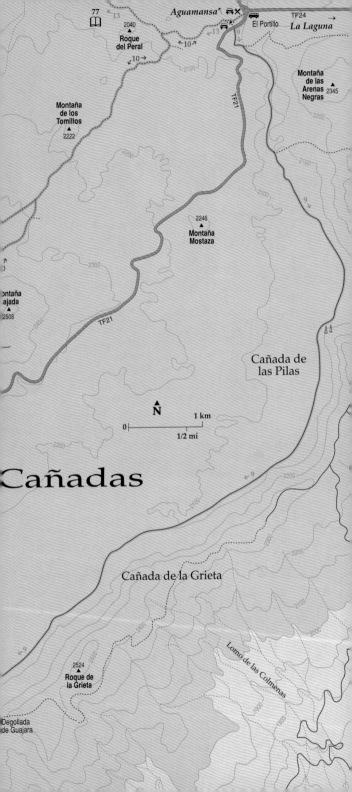

77

Aguamansa

El Portillo

TF24

La Laguna

13

13

10

10

2040

**Roque
del Peral**

2100

TF21

**Montaña
de las
Arenas
Negras**
▲ 2345

**Montaña
de los
Tomillos**
▲
2222

2200

2100

2200

2100

2200

9

2300

2246
▲
**Montaña
Mostaza**

2100

**ontaña
ajada**
▲
2508

2200

TF21

2300

**Cañada de
las Pilas**

▲
N

0

1 km

1/2 mi

2200

Cañadas

9

2200

2100

2200

Cañada de la Grieta

2200

9

2524
▲
**Roque de
la Grieta**

Lomo de las Colmenas

**Degollada
de Guajara**

notice board stands at the foot of the sandy path, which is clear throughout. From down here, the side of El Teide seems to be split vertically: the left is clothed in dark lava flow and the right in light crusty pumice.

At **2h35min** the **Refugio de Altavista** is no longer a dot on the mountainside. You're there, 3270m/10,725ft up. Your path continues up behind the shelter, to the left, through a landscape covered in stones and chunks of rock. Less than 20 minutes up from the *refugio*, turn off right for the **Cueva del Hielo**, a minute away (the turn-off is marked by a small pile of stones and usually a signpost). Snow used to be packed in this large sunken pit, to make ice. A springy metal ladder allows entry to this den: *take care!* Inside the cave are many stalactites.

Returning to the main path, the smooth volcanic cone of Montaña Mostaza (Walk 9) stands out below. Soon the walk levels out a bit. If a wind is blowing, as it often is, this is where it will be in full force. You quickly come to a T-junction, where a right turn leads to the **Mirador de la Fortaleza**. After enjoying the view over the Orotava Valley, return to the main path and keep right. The way becomes a paved path twisting through a wild sea of rock. It takes you past the path to the summit, straight to the CABLE CAR STATION/BAR (**3h25min**). Rising puffs of steam betray concealed holes in the ground. Whiffs of sulphur waft by. If your hands need warming, hold them over these steaming holes. The drop in temperature causes small droplets of condensation, and strings of frozen water crystallise on the rocks; when the sun's rays catch these droplets, the slope appears diamond-studded.

To climb to the peak, show your permit to one of the park rangers and return to the ascent path. It's a further 20 minutes to the SUMMIT (**3h45min**). A small crater (80m/yds diameter) lies just below the peak. Here the soft colours of an ice cream parlour surround you: banana, peach melba, strawberry, mocha, pistachio. On a clear day, your view encompasses four islands — La Gomera, Gran Canaria, El Hierro and La Palma.

Before boarding the cable car for the return, follow the path that heads below the station. A 20-minute walk takes you to the **Mirador de Pico Viejo** (**4h40min**), for a perfect view over this massive crater (800m diameter!), before you retrace your steps to the bar (**4h50min**).

If you are returning to the TF21 on foot, retrace your steps, allowing just under three hours for the descent (**7h45min**).

11 ROQUES DE GARCIA AND LA CATEDRAL

Map pages 68-69

Distance: 4km/2.5mi; 1h25min

Grade: moderate, with ascents totalling 150m/500ft (the final ascent is steep and slippery)

Equipment: walking boots, sunhat, fleece, rain-/windproof, gloves, picnic, water

How to get there and return: 🚌 348 from Puerto to/from the Parador de Las Cañadas (Timetable 5); journey time 2h; or 🚗: park at the Mirador de la Ruleta, opposite the *parador*.

This hike has got to be the gem of Las Cañadas. It's short, it's very accessible, and it's a geological treat. But be prepared for lots of company on this circuit round the Roques (Picnic 11). Before starting the walk, climb to the

God's Finger, passed at the start of the walk, with El Teide in the background and retama *brightening the path*

Mirador de la Ruleta, a fine viewpoint overlooking the Cañada Llano de Ucanca. The gigantic fractured rock rising up in front of you, out of this *cañada*, is called La Catedral. You'll walk in its shadow on the return leg of the hike. This is a waymarked walk (Walk 3 in the park management scheme), so you'll see small plaques bearing this number.

Returning from the *mirador,* **start out** by following the designated path heading north from the ROUNDABOUT, alongside the eroded rocks. The solitary rock pillar on your left, featured in all the brochures, is called 'God's Finger'. Soon you come to another good lookout point. From here your path is bordered by stones. The path narrows as it passes between a ridge of rough, jagged rock on the right and the *roques* on the left.

Lumps of *pahoehoe* lava begin rising up around you as you approach the **Roques Blancos**, the last of the Roques de García. The lava flow is usually a smooth stream of distorted, rolling hillocks and hollows; parts of it resemble cord, or coils of rope — hence the name. The ropey lava flow is formed on the thin crust of the stream, either by the movement of liquified lava underneath, or by the sliding of the crust where it has thrust up into a hillock. The more common lava up here is the 'A-A' (block lava) — large scoriaceous masses of jagged, fragmented rock.

La Torre Blanca (the White Tower) is a solitary rock met at the **25min**-mark. North of here are many caves, the Cuevas de Los Roques (now out of bounds to walkers, due to damage to plants and the ropey lava). These caves were formed millennia ago when the surface crust thickened but the lava underneath continued to run, spreading

The entrance to one of the smaller caves (taken before they were off-limits), opening off a flow of easily recognised ropey lava

The Roques de García, seen on the descent towards the Cañada Llano de Ucanca

its tentacles. When these streams subsided, they left an extensive network of tunnels and caves — some of them extending up to 1000m/ 3300ft back into the slope!

Continuing on the circuit, you quickly reach a 'balcony' *mirador* offering a last look over the lake-sized Cañada Llano de Ucanca. From here cairns mark your descent towards the *cañada*. The path swings back to the left and you circle behind the rocks, in the setting shown above. Rocks of all dimensions rear up before you — jagged upthrusts … sheets of rock … twisted fingers. Note, too, the 'waterfall' of ropey lava that pours through a gap in the rocks. Look back! With the ever-present El Teide in the background, and the pastel-coloured rocks in the foreground, you won't be able to put your camera away. A spectrum of volcanic hues saturates the landscape. If you're lucky enough to catch the *retama* in bloom, the view is even more spectacular.

Soon you're in the shadow of the imposing rock, **La Catedral**. Rising over 100m/330ft from the plain, with rocky spire-like pinnacles, it is well named. Here the hard work begins: you climb straight up to the car park — a 25-minute slog. Along the way, a slight detour to a massive rock on the right affords another fine view over the *cañada*, before you return to the CAR PARK (**1h25min**).

12 MONTAÑA DE GUAJARA

Map pages 68-69; see also photograph page 19

Distance: 9.5km/6mi; 4h30min

Grade: moderate-strenuous climb of 600m/1950ft. The descent (via the Degollada de Ucanca) is *only recommended for experienced and adventurous hikers*: the slippery path is vertiginous and involves clambering over boulders and crossing landslides. As an alternative, you can return the way you came. *Do not attempt in unsettled weather. Note:* You may prefer to do the walk in reverse; the faded grey paint waymarking is more easily seen when *ascending* via the Ucanca Pass.

Equipment: walking boots, sunhat, fleece, windproof, long trousers, gloves, thick socks, picnic, water

How to get there and return: 🚌 348 from Puerto to/from the Parador de las Cañadas (Timetable 5); journey time 2h; or 🚗: park at the *parador*

Shorter walk: *parador — Degollada de Guajara — parador:* 8.5km/ 5.3mi; 2h40min. Moderate climb and descent of under 250m/820ft; access and equipment as above. Follow the main walk for 1h30min; return the same way.

Guajara is Tenerife's third highest mountain, standing at 2717m/8910ft. This is an easy, straightforward climb, offering superb views down into the crater of Las Cañadas. As you ascend Guajara's back, the southern coastal plain unravels in a haze below. The descent via the Degollada de Ucanca is exhilarating, if a little hair-raising!

Start out at the **Parador de las Cañadas**. Your destination is the prominent mountain protruding out of the crater wall southeast of the *parador*. Head for the main road, and turn left along it. After 50m/yds along the main road, turn left on a gravel track. Then veer right on a path alongside the rocky ridge. This path takes you to a tarred road in a few minutes. Turn left and pass through the control barrier, onto the Las Cañadas track. A fascinating formation of pink and yellow rocks rises just in front of you. The pastel colours give this fine natural sculpture its name — **Piedras Amarillas** ('Yellow Stones'; Picnic 12; photograph page 19). Behind them, you cross a small *cañada* (gravel plain). Another *cañada* follows. Here Guajara — the bastion of the encircling walls — is seen at its best, rising 500m/1650ft from the crater floor. Splashes of yellow lichen, like paint daubs, decorate the higher rock

View down over the parador, the Piedras Amarillas and the Roques de García

74

faces. In spring, *taginaste rojo* — some as tall as 3m/10ft — add bold strokes of red to this canvas.

Your ascent begins at the **50min**-mark. *Attention:* it's not very obvious. It lies not far beyond the turn-off left to Montaña de Majuá and the cable car, and about 70m/yds past a bend dominated by a towering wall of rock. Two small cairns, on your right, announce it. Once underway, the path is easily seen. You reach the edge of the crater at the **Degollada de Guajara**; 2373m/7785ft; **1h30min**), where a high-level path comes in from El Portillo. The views are magnificent. The tones are the most dramatic aspect of this landscape, as they flow into and across each other. *(The Shorter walk turns back here).*

Ignore the small path branching off right at the pass; just continue straight over, beneath bleached pumice cliffs on the right. Gran Canaria seems surprisingly close from this vantage point. A little over five minutes along, you come to a fork (there *may* also be a metal pole here): keep right for Guajara. (The path to the left leads to Vilaflor via the famous 'moon landscape' — a hike described in *Landscapes of Southern Tenerife and La Gomera*.) An eroded watercourse briefly becomes your path. Small cairns help to keep you on route. The way eases out as it swings across the *retama*- and *codéso*-patched slope. Around here the path fades from time to time, so be prepared to search out those cairns. Don't veer left; keep straight uphill, and the path will reassert itself.

El Teide slowly reappears until it is seen in its full magnificence when you reach the Guajara SUMMIT (**2h 30min**), marked by a trig point. There's also a rock enclosure here — a good picnic shelter on a windy winter's day, but it gets crowded. The panorama from Guajara's

summit can only be matched by that from El Teide. *(If you're taking the same route back, your return path begins a little to the left of the rock-pen. While the descent is much easier than the ascent, take it very slowly down the stretch of slippery pumice.)*

To descend via the Degollada de Ucanca, face El Teide and find your path just to the right of the rock enclosure. From this vantage point it *appears* to just fly off the cliffs, but it swings back to the left, hugging the escarpment wall. (There is a clear cairned path all the way down, but it rebraids itself from time to time. The faded grey paint waymarking is more easily seen if ascending.) Setting off, your way heads down through large boulders. After a few minutes, the path veers right to a spectacular cliff-top viewpoint, where you look straight down onto the Degollada de Guajara. But your route heads to the left, so return to the left side of the promontory, keeping close to the escarpment wall. You'll have to scramble down and over rock, often on all fours. Magnificent views lie ahead all the way down. But be sure to *stop* to take them all in.

About 15 minutes downhill, you're just at the foot of these towering cliffs. *Taginaste* (see page 56) flourishes amidst the rock. The Llano de Ucanca is the expansive lake of gravel that lies on the edge of a dark lava flow. A little further on you're edging along the narrowest section of the shelf, a short vertiginous stretch. After the descent eases somewhat, you cross two slippery pumice sections of hillside — other narrow and vertiginous sections. The left side of the crater is in full view; its walls are very impressive.

The path later descends a lateral ridge, to a clump of stumpy pines (about 45 minutes below the summit). Walk through the pines, to continue downhill on the left side of the ridge. Just after crossing a small flat area and ascending a little, you reach the **Degollada de Ucanca** (**3h30min**), marked by a splash of white paint and a small cairn. Ignore the path climbing to the left here.

Once over the pass, the path briefly descends to the left before swinging back to the right to zigzag down the hillside. The colours in the immediate landscape are a stunning mixture of green, yellow, pink, mauve and white, while over to your right are the Piedras Amarillas. Coming onto a dazzling patch of white and yellow hillside, the path veers right and soon takes you to the road, from where you follow the path directly opposite, back to the **Parador de las Cañadas** (**4h30min**).

13 EL PORTILLO • PIEDRA DE LOS PASTORES • GALERIA ALMAGRE Y CABEZON • CHANAJIGA • PALO BLANCO

See also photograph pages 80-81 **Distance:** 15km/9.3mi; 4h30min

Grade: moderate-strenuous descent of 1450m/4750ft; some sections are very steep and *hazardous if wet*.

Equipment: walking boots, sunhat, fleece, rain-/windproof, picnic, water

How to get there: 348 from Puerto to El Portillo (Timetable 5); journey time 1h

To return: 347 from Palo Blanco to La Orotava (Timetable 10); journey time 30min; *change to* 350 to Puerto (Timetable 3); journey time 30min

Short walk: El Portillo — Choza Cruz de Fregel — El Portillo: 7km/ 4.3mi; 2h. Easy descents/ascents of under 100m/330ft; access/ return on 348 as above; equipment as above, but stout shoes will suffice. Follow the main walk for 1h and return the same way.

Alternative walk: La Fortaleza: 13km/8mi; 4h. Access, equipment and grade as Short walk (ascents/descents of about 200m/650ft). Do the Short walk but, from Cruz de Fregel visit three *miradors*. First, with La Fortaleza to your right, walk to the viewpoint at the end of the *cañada*. Retrace steps and ascend back to the *degollada* on the path rising west-northwest, then take the forestry track to the left, followed by a path, to a viewpoint at the end of the rocks (but on top of them). Again retrace steps and turn right up to the viewpoint on the highest point.

Three scenic stretches make this walk: the volcanic world that lies at the foot of El Teide, the sunken lake of fine gravel just before you leave it, and the wooded western slopes of the Orotava Valley.

On your bus journey up to El Portillo, you'll pass the famous Margarita de Piedra — a basaltic rock formation in the shape of a daisy (drawing page 12). You may also see piles of pine needles by the road, awaiting collection. They're used as packing material for easily-bruised fruit.

Start out at **El Portillo**: follow the path behind the RESTAURANT, keeping right at a fork almost immediately. Pass a fork off to the left in two minutes and, at the next fork, keep right (or first go left, to the Las Cañadas Visitors' Centre, open 09.15-16.00). Continue west on this path, intermittently waymarked with the numbers 1 and 6 (the park management's numbering scheme). This pretty path (Picnic 13b; photograph below) ends in **20min**, when you meet a T-junction and turn right. Soon, from a slight rise,

you have a fine view of the **Roque del Peral** (signposted) on your left. Ignore all turn-offs along this route.

An exciting change takes place as you descend to an unexpected, sunken 'lake' of fine-gravelled pumice and sand. Your feet will assure you it's not solely sand — as it at first appears. This is **Cañada de los Guancheros**. Cross the *cañada,* keeping near the right-hand wall. A few minutes across, beyond a blade of rock jutting out of the wall, climb a path bearing right, to a small cluster of pines that huddle in the **Degollada del Cedro**, a pass to the right of **La Fortaleza**. Here you come upon the **Cruz de Fregel** recreation area (**1h**; photograph top left), where three wooden crosses sit in a tiny chapel. Unless someone has replaced them, there are no seats left to sit and enjoy your barbecue, and the *choza* has collapsed.

Cruz de Fregel (top), La Fortaleza (middle), and (bottom): the path from the visitors' centre (Picnic 13b)

From here follow the forestry track downhill to the right, ignoring a turn-off climbing to the left just beyond the chapel. A couple of minutes along, turn left on a wide path, marked by a small cairn. The odd *sendero turístico* sign may still confirm the way. Ten minutes further down, you cross a U-bend in the forestry track, and 10 minutes later this track is crossed again. Continue straight downhill, ignoring the track. Soon you join another track and swing right to cross a small *barranco*.

You enter a wide FIRE-BREAK (**1h50min**) on the western side of this ridge and join a second track coming from the right. Continue downhill through the frayed clearing, with some striking views over the whole Orotava Valley.

Beyond a small shrine on the left, you soon come to the roofless **Choza Piedra de los Pastores** (the Shepherds' Rock Shelter; **2h20min**). Here signs point in all directions.

Below the *choza* the T-junction is marked with a sign 'Las Cañadas' to the right. Turn *left* here and, a few metres downhill, find that your track is signposted 'CHANAJIGA'. After about 100m/yds, on a bend to the left, take a path to the right, again signposted to Chanajiga. This beautiful old woodland path zigzags down the side of a steep ridge above the Orotava Valley. After 20 minutes you cross a track and pick up the ongoing path opposite. There may be a lot of fallen trees on this stretch — proof of the severe storms that sometimes rage through these mountains.

Ten minutes later you leave the forest and pass **Galería La Zarza** (**2h50min**; see pages 44-45). Here the path widens out into a track, and there is likely to be forestry work going on as trees are cleared by the environmental authorities. The type of pine being removed is *not* the Canary pine, but the *Pinus insignis* — a species from the Spanish mainland introduced by General Franco in the 1950s. It is totally unfit for these regions, being a very weak pine, unable to withstand strong winds. During winter storms the trees just break up like match-sticks or toppled over because their roots are superficial. For a short time after clearance takes place the affected area looks very barren and ugly, but within a few months the indigenous vegetation regenerates.

Follow the track down towards Chanajiga. (Ignore the track joining from the right a minute along.) In 20 minutes, at a junction, head left to **Chanajiga** (**3h30min**; Picnic 13a). It's about an hour from here to **Palo Blanco** (**4h30min**): use the notes for Walk 14 from the 2h45min-point (page 82) and the map on pages 84-85.

14 ICOD EL ALTO • LA CORONA • CHANAJIGA • PALO BLANCO

Map pages 84-85
Distance: 10.5km/6.5mi; 3h45min (or 4h15min to Los Realejos)
Grade: strenuous, with an initial climb of 700m/2300ft and a steep descent of 600m/2000ft
Equipment: stout shoes (walking boots preferable), sunhat, fleece, rain/windproof, picnic, water
How to get there: 🚌 354 from Puerto to Icod el Alto (Timetable 4); journey time 35min; alight at the ***first stop*** past the Mirador de El Lance.
To return: 🚌 347 from Palo Blanco to La Orotava (Timetable 10); journey time 30min; *change to* 🚌 350 to Puerto (Timetable 3); journey time 30min

Shorter walk: Icod — Mirador El Asomadero — Icod: 6km/3.8mi; 2h 10min. Strenuous ascent/descent of 500m/1650ft; access/equipment as above (or 🚗). Follow the main walk for 1h25min; return the same way.

If you've done Walk 5, you've explored the Orotava Valley from the east. On this walk, you'll get to know the west. This trek is one continuous panorama, where your views stretch far beyond the eastern escarpment. The hike ascends a ridge. And then the rural descent, equally as steep, lets you absorb the country atmosphere as you follow narrow lanes through terraced fields.

On the bus journey to Icod, you have an opportunity to see one of the big dragon trees. This one stands on the far side of the ravine, just out of Los Realejos.

Press the button *immediately* after passing the first bus stop in Icod el Alto, which is adjacent to the Mirador de El Lance. Your stop is the *next* one. Off the bus, walk downhill to a BUS SHELTER on the opposite side of the road, where **the walk begins**. Some 15m/yds beyond the shelter, climb the lane between the houses (closed to motor traffic). You come to a road climbing steeply up from the TF342 (CALLE EL LANCE). Keep right uphill here, quickly leaving

Descending through spring crops at Palo Blanco, near the end of the walk

Icod. After about **20min** of huffing and puffing, you turn off left on a tarred lane — the first turn-off beyond the groups of houses, about 800m/0.5mi uphill (just at the end of a high, wire fence on the right). This lane reverts to concrete, then dirt track, and soon takes you to the **Mirador La Corona** (**35min**; Picnic 14), where there is also a shrine and host of antennae. The view from here is a sample of what lies further up. Once you've absorbed it all, and worked out where each village lies, head up the ridge from the top part of the *mirador*. From here, a wide, dusty farm and forestry track leads you straight up past more antennae. Ignore all the tracks that turn off across the hillside to the right. (If you are ever in doubt, always follow the *edge* of the ridge.)

Less than 20 minutes up, at an intersection, continue straight uphill (the middle track, an overgrown fire-break). From here on, this fire-break is your guide. Around 10 minutes from the intersection, you meet a forestry track which completes its curve and veers off to the right. Another, smaller track heads off left round the eastern face of the ridge. Again, keep straight uphill, by following the middle track. Fifteen minutes later, you join the main forestry track on a bend, then immediately leave it by forking left on another track that cuts up the edge of the escarpment. (The main track now winds up through

scrub, over on your right.) Another magnificent view-point, the **Mirador El Asomadero** (with the last antennae), draws you to a halt (**1h25min**). You're overlooking farmland, a quilted patchwork of fields in the upper valley. Straight in front of you is Palo Blanco, an elongated rural settlement, clearly identified by the school. (*The Shorter walk turns back here.*)

Just past the *mirador* a concrete lane appears, and you follow it to the left. Three minutes later, at an intersection, keep left uphill. A further three minutes brings you to another intersection, where you again keep left. When you next meet the main track, follow it uphill to the right for a couple of minutes, before turning off left uphill again (on a slightly overgrown path). Then you come to an *important junction,* signposted for CHANAJIGA/REALEJOS, where you again keep left. From here on, clear views accompany you all the way to the signposted **Mirador de Sergio**. From here it's only a couple of hundred metres to **Chanajiga** (**2h45min**), an extensive recreation area. Walk 13 comes in here (from Piedra de los Pastores).

To make for Palo Blanco, follow the gravel road from the picnic area for 300m/yds, to a signposted junction, where you turn left on a tarred road. About 100m/yds downhill, on a curve, you come to a CAIRN on the left and turn off left on a track. Walking downhill, look up to the left, to see the track that brought you down the mountain-side (it's the lower one). A minute past two concrete farm sheds, you join a tarred country lane, where you turn left and continue downhill. On meeting a road cutting across in front of you, cross it and continue downhill on the steep tarred lane. This leads you to another lane, where you turn right. Ten minutes further downhill, you pass through a junction and keep straight ahead. This very steep descent takes you through authentic rural landscapes, with hidden courtyards, flower beds, children ... and dogs galore. You pass the SCHOOL on the right and continue down to the main road in **Palo Blanco** (**3h 45min**), which cuts across in front of you. The BUS STOP is at the junction. Buses here in Palo Blanco are infrequent. But if you continue straight over the road, half an hour downhill, in Realejo Alto, you can pick up a bus to Puerto. (When you come to the first main street (with shops), veer right, then take the first left: the bus stop is in this street.)

15 ICOD EL ALTO • EL LAGAR • LA GUANCHA

Distance: 18km/11.2mi; 7h30min

Grade: very strenuous and long, with a steep ascent of 1000m/3300ft at the start and a descent of 1000m/3300ft at the end. To avoid the initial climb, take a taxi to El Lagar and use the map to walk from there to Icod (ie, do the walk in reverse).

Equipment: stout shoes (walking boots preferable in wet weather), sunhat, fleece, rain-/windproof, long trousers, picnic, water

How to get there: 🚌 354 from Puerto to Icod el Alto (Timetable 4); journey time 35min; or 🚗 to Icod el Alto
To return: 🚌 354 from La Guancha to Puerto (as above), or back to Icod el Alto to pick up your car

Shorter walk: Icod el Alto — bridge — Icod el Alto: 8km/5mi; 3h50min. Strenuous climb/descent of 800m/2600ft; equipment and access/return as main walk. Follow the main walk to the bridge just beyond the 2h30min-point and return the same way.

High terraced slopes, rich in cultivation, lead you higher still, into the confines of the forest. On this walk, contact with Canarians is a certainty. If you don't speak Spanish, at least smile and say 'Buenos días', but if your Spanish is good enough, don't be afraid to stop for a chat — the local farmers especially will be delighted to pass the time of day with you.

See Walk 14, page 80, to alight at your bus stop and **start the walk**. At the **20min**-point, where Walk 14 heads left, continue uphill to the right. In about **30min** a small hamlet sits on the nose of a ridge over to your right. At this point, take the narrow path on the right (about 20m/yds beyond the last house, on a bend in the road). At the lowest point in this path, ignore a fork to the left. Cross the tarred road leading to the Mirador La Corona and head up the steep road almost opposite. This road soon reverts to track, which ascends alongside a ravine. Rich alluvial plots step the slope on the right. Ignore all farm tracks left and right.

Twenty minutes up this track, you meet the end of a tarred road and turn right along it. Some 400m/yds along, turn left up a track, towards a lone house not far above (a short-cut). Meeting the end of another road, turn left uphill on its continuation — a concrete lane, which will take you almost straight uphill to the La Guancha forestry track. Montaña de Taco, a volcanic cone rising out of Buenavista's coastal plain, can be seen from here and, on clear days, La Palma is visible on the horizon.

After about 20 minutes ignore a track branching off to the right. Five minutes later, at a junction, keep right. At the next junction (which is just around the bend), the concrete lane becomes a dirt track. Take the track that

heads up the left-hand side of the ravine here — not the chained-off, *'Prohibido'* track, but the *next* one. Don't cross the ravine. During the next 20 minutes, keep straight uphill, ignoring side-tracks. El Teide is before you, rising above the pines, and heather cloaks the immediate slopes.

Within **2h30min** you reach the LA GUANCHA FORESTRY TRACK and turn right, soon crossing a high bridge. *(The Shorter walk turns back from this point.)* You now follow this track, without turning off. Pass a fork off to the right and come immediately to a T-junction: go left here. The track now ascends for a while. Cross straight over an inter-section at **Los Campeches** and, later, ignore another track forking off to the right. At **Lomo del Astillero (3h35min)**, you pass a small SHRINE set back off the track. Keep an eye on the WATER PIPE beside the track from here on. A few minutes later, ignore the turn-off to the right; keep following the track with the water pipe. Go straight over at the next junction and, 10 minutes later, ignore forks to

the left and right. About 1 km further on, ignore two tracks descending from the left. At about this point you part company with the water pipe, which now cuts across the hillside. A few minutes later you pass through a major junction, keeping straight ahead for 'ZONA RECREATIVA EL LAGAR'. This brings you to **Campamento Barranco de la Arena**, a campsite and picnic area (**4h40min**).

Leaving the campsite, follow the track that cuts *straight through* the picnic grounds. A couple of minutes along, you meet a track coming from the left. Follow the track to the right for 20m/yds, then take the path forking down to the left, through rocks and into the pines. In 10 minutes you rejoin the track and follow it to the left for 50m/yds. Then you rejoin your path, on the left, and head back into the woods. Ignore all the faint turn-offs; keep straight downhill. The track and path run parallel from time to time, and a small WATER PIPE accompanies you. Then the somewhat-overgrown path rises, nestling into the slope of a ridge. Shortly you cross another low ridge: ahead of you is a superb panorama — the two humps on the horizon are La Palma. The path descends away from the pipe and soon another superb view beckons, as you begin to descend the left-hand side of a steep ridge, in the setting shown below. When you eventually rejoin the track, follow it down to the left and then turn right.

The **El Lagar** *zona recreativa* (**5h40min**; Picnic 15) is 100m/yds below. From here you will follow the track for a short time, but then woodcutters' paths will take you to the beautifully-sited village of La Guancha, strung along a ridge. Start down the track from El Lagar; it is signposted 'LA GUANCHA'. Around five minutes downhill, ignore the San Juan/Los Realejos turn-off (on the right). Less than five minutes later, rounding a sweeping bend, you'll see a ridge sloping down to the left. Take the path

El Teide dominates the waves of pines.

running along the top of it. It's not very clear, but just keep straight downhill. (If you miss this turn-off, you'll have another opportunity to join the path some 50m/yds downhill — see map.) On crossing the forestry track, find the path immediately opposite. Several minutes later, you cross the track again: the path continues opposite. Cross the track again in barely two minutes and continue downhill through a particularly scenic part of the forest (the bottom of this path is slightly overgrown). You leave the woodland path again at a junction: almost exactly at the point where two tracks meet, your path re-enters the wood. Continue downhill into the bottom of a shallow gulley, ignoring faint side-paths. Late in the afternoon, streams of light flicker through the dark shadows.

The path swings right and crosses over the crest. You leave the shady forest, cross the track, and enter a patch of pines. A good five minutes downhill, you cross the track again. Here veer slightly left onto an old forestry track and, 10m/yds along it, pick up the path again, dipping off to the right. The path joins an old track, and the gurgle of fast-running water from a *canal* announces the next track crossing. Go down through trees and moss.

You soon meet a tarred road: cross it and continue through pines and heather. A little way along this track, ignore the path branching off to the left. A *canal* passes under the track as it curves to the right. A minute later, go left through a small gap in the dense vegetation, following a rocky path. It takes you to another, wider path, running above cultivated plots. Thick, tightly-woven moss carpets the shady corners of this path. The forest continues down past you on the left. The road is below, and the town of La Guancha is at last nearby. The sea is glistening over the pines. Enjoy these final far-reaching coastal views.

About 10 minutes down this path, you meet a junction above a lane, in a very picturesque rural setting. Descend the concrete lane, past vineyards and orchards. Streams of white dwellings come into sight, extending across the escarpment and dribbling down the ridges. Two minutes down the lane, on a sharp bend, fork right on a path (just above a large CIRCULAR WATER TANK). Keep right and come to a BASKETBALL COURT. Turn left to the tarred road. The main road (TF342) can be seen from here, passing through the centre of **La Guancha**. To get there, turn right down the road, go left at the T-junction and, three minutes later, descend steps on the left. Turn right on the main road. The BUS STOP is some 200m/yds ahead (**7h30min**).

16 LA MONTAÑETA • LAS ARENAS NEGRAS • LOS PARTIDOS DE FRANQUIS • ERJOS • LOS SILOS

Distance: 16.5km/10.3mi; 5h10min

Grade: fairly easy but long, with an ascent of 300m/1000ft at the start and an overall descent of 1200m/4000ft — a little tough on knees.

Note: Climbing Montaña Negra is no longer permitted. Please help conserve this beautiful natural site. Unfortunately, many tourists do not; some because they don't understand the signs, others don't give a hoot!

Equipment: walking boots, sunhat, fleece, rain-/windproof, picnic, water

How to get there: 🚌 363 from Puerto to the bus station at Icod de los Vinos (Timetable 6); journey time 45min; at the bus station *change to* 🚌 360 and ask for 'Ermita de San Francisco'. (Timetable 8); journey time 35min

To return: 🚌 363 from Los Silos to Puerto (Timetable 6); journey time 1h10min

Shorter walks

1 La Montañeta — Montaña Negra — La Montañeta: 8.5km/5.3mi; 2h30min. Fairly easy ascent/descent of 300m/1000ft; access as above or by 🚗; return on the same buses; equipment as above, but stout shoes will suffice. Follow the main walk to the El Volcán Negro cairn and return via the short-cut path just in front of it (see map).

2 La Montañeta — Las Arenas Negras — Los Partidos de Franquis — TF82: 10.5km/6.5mi; 3h. Fairly easy, with an ascent of 300m/1000ft at the start; access and equipment as above, but stout shoes will suffice. Return on 🚌 325 from the San José de los Llanos turn-off to Puerto (Timetable 16); journey time 1h15min. Or return on 🚌 460 to Icod de los Vinos (Timetable 7); journey time 40min; *change to* 🚌 363 from Icod to Puerto (Timetable 6); journey time 45min. Follow the walk up to the San José de los Llanos road, where the main walk turns right. Here turn left for the TF82, 15min away — see short-cut route on the map.

This is one of my favourite hikes, packed with spectacular scenery. The black mound of Las Arenas Negras and its surrounding sands provides us with the volcanic touch. Out of the sands, we pass through wild, open country, high above a plain. A brief transition to lush grassy slopes follows, as we desend. Later, crossing a plain, we are enveloped in a forest of *escobón*. And on the final leg, down a hidden valley, an old path leads us through a great tangle of vegetation, first through laurel forest and then down a defile with a wealth of exotic plant life.

The walk starts at **La Montañeta**, on the path behind the 'Respete la Naturaleza' sign, just uphill from the bus stop and across the road from a chapel, the **Ermita San Francisco**. Climb the crest directly behind the sign. In five minutes meet an old track and turn left uphill. Cross the Los Llanos road and, shortly after, the forestry track to Las Arenas Negras. Ignore two turn-offs left three minutes later. Come out of the trees (**20min**), meet a three-way junction and go straight ahead on the main forestry track.

Las Arenas Negras (Picnic 16, Car tour 3)

Having ignored a faint fork off to the right and another to the left, you reach **Las Arenas Negras** (**40min**; Picnic 16).

Continue up the track. Immediately upon entering the picnic area and children's playground, turn left alongside the low stone wall. Just before a stone building with a tiled roof, turn uphill to the forest track (PISTA DEL CANAL) and follow it to the right. Just over 20 minutes up, keep an eye out for two small concrete buildings in the trees on your right. They are perched on one of the island's longest and most important watercourses, the **Canal Vergara** (**1h 05min**). **Galería Vergara Alta**, and the *canal* it feeds, are responsible for a large supply of water conveyed to the southern side of the island; the system has been operating since the early 1950s. This gallery goes back some 3.5 kilometres (over two miles) into the mountainside, and they're still excavating! Fork right on the track just below the *canal* (walking atop the watercourse is not permitted, as signs clearly indicate all along the *canal*). Head back towards the volcanic fields of black sand, into the alluring confines of Montaña Negra. This stark enclosed landscape comes ablaze as the sand shimmers and the encircling pines flicker under the bright sun.

Before long, you find the trees thinning out and the sands opening up ahead. En route you pass through a barrier. Clusters of sharp grey rock attract your attention with their patchy coating of thick rusty-orange lichen. **Montaña Negra** is now beside you on the right. *(If you're doing Shorter walk 1, note this point. Your way, which has narrowed to a path, veers sharply left here in front of the mountain. For your return, take the path striking right off this sharp turn, which will take you back to the picnic*

grounds.) Pines, planted out symmetrically in a hollow immediately ahead, catch the eye. Continuing to the left, you see a long rough tail of crusted lava heading seaward. Just past Montaña Negra, you reach a cairn, '**El Volcán Negro**' (**1h35min**). *(Shorter walk 1 turns back here.)*

Heading on, you briefly re-enter the pines, then exit through a control barrier. Soon a magnificent viewpoint greets you. On a clear day, La Gomera can be seen clearly — even its villages! To the right lie the twin humps of La Palma. Los Llanos betrays its secluded location on the far right. Approaching 30 minutes from Montaña Negra, at a junction of four tracks, turn right. Keep downhill, ignoring minor turn-offs. About 10 minutes down ignore a track to the right; make your way across a plain forested in *escobón* — a beautiful sight in March when the trees are in bloom. Again, ignore all minor turn-offs. At the next two junctions (the first being **Corral Nueva**), keep straight on.

The hamlet of **Los Partidos de Franquis** is barely noticeable — it's overgrown and all but deserted. But hidden away here is a lovely small countryside hotel, the Caserío Los Partidos' (see page 6). As you leave the basin, more signs of cultivation appear. Beyond the hamlet, the ROAD TO SAN JOSÉ DE LOS LLANOS cuts across the track (**2h40min**); follow it to the right. *(But for Shorter walk 2, turn left and refer to the map below for short cuts.)* A good ten minutes along the road, turn left for Erjos. Beyond the

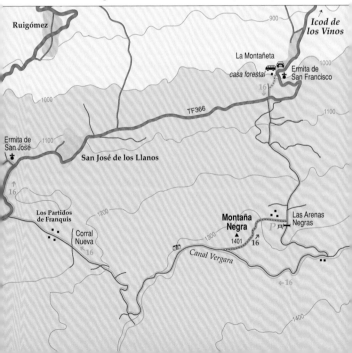

Aeonium nobile

Ranunculus cortusfolius

Red-flowering tabaiba (Euphorbia atropurpurea)

Canary bellflower (Campanula canariensis)

Vinagrera (Rumex lunaria)

Ermita de San José, head left on the tarred road. Coming into **Erjos**, keep right, then go left just before the SCHOOL. At the junction, turn right. Cross the TF82 and head down to the CHURCH (**3h20min**).

At the church, turn sharp left and, just over the crest, turn right for 'LOS SILOS' (but the walking time of 3h30min on the sign is an exaggeration!). When the street ends, continue on a path down into the *barranco*. Keep straight on past the houses, several of which belong to those enjoying an 'alternative lifestyle'. The path is clear throughout; ignore all turn-offs. The *barranco* floor is overgrown, with neglected plots. Soon you disappear into the woods. Sagging stone walls with moss-covered rocks flank the path. It's deathly quiet down here. Fifty minutes from Erjos you pass a beautiful OLD DWELLING in an overgrown garden behind stone walls (**4h10min**).

Little houses on the *barranco* wall over to the right are the first signs of the isolated hamlet of **Las Cuevas Negras**. Most of the small stone houses are buried in hillside vegetation. Ignore a path to the left near a *'sendero'* signpost. Crossing the *barranco,* you encounter a few more derelict buildings and pass a path ascending to the houses. This is a delightful spot. The plains of Los Silos appear through the V in the valley, which narrows to a defile of high jagged walls. The path steepens, and you pass below an impressive rockface. Stepping down out of the *barranco,* you come to luxuriant garden plots, orchards, and banana groves. A rough concrete lane takes you out of the valley. Seven minutes down the lane, you cross the *barranco* at a ford. Some 100m/yds further on, turn left on a path that crosses the *barranco* via a small wooden bridge. Another bridge follows, and you then turn right down a lane to the valley floor. The BUS STOP in **Los Silos** is at the junction of the bypass road and Calle Susana, just by the CHURCH (**5h10min**).

17 ERJOS • LAS LAGUNETAS • EL PALMAR

See map pages 90-91; see photograph page 26
Distance: 10.5km/6.5mi; 3h25min
Grade: fairly easy descent of 500m/1650ft on tracks
Equipment: stout shoes, sunhat, fleece, windproof, water, picnic
How to get there: 🚌 325 from Puerto to Erjos (Timetable 16); journey time 1h15min
To return: 🚌 366 from El Palmar to Buenavista (Timetable 11); journey time 15min; *change to* 🚌 363 for Puerto (Timetable 6); journey time 50min

Alternative walks

1 **Erjos — Los Lavaderos — Erjos**: 13km/8mi; 4h10min. Moderate, but with a tiring ascent of 300m/1000ft at the end. Equipment as above, but hiking boots recommended. Access/return by 🚌 325 (as above) or 🚗. Or return on 🚌 460 to Icod de los Vinos, then *change to* 🚌 363 for Puerto (as Walk 16, page 88). Follow the main walk to the *second* Las Moradas turn-off (1h40min). Keep right here, and continue down the track for a further 35 minutes. Watch for an abandoned concrete building above the track and, two minutes beyond it, turn right uphill on a path, climbing the bed of a *barranco*. Three minutes up, meet a path cutting around the hillside and turn left along it. Follow this path all the way up to the Erjos/El Palmar forestry track, 35 minutes uphill. Now retrace your outgoing route back to Erjos, 1h25min away.

2 **Erjos — Los Lavaderos — Los Silos:** 10km/6mi; 3h35min. Fairly easy, but with a descent of 900m/3000ft — a little tough on the knees. Equipment and access as main walk; return as Walk 21 (page 105). Follow the walk below to the 1h40min-point, then pick up Walk 21 at its 2h25min-point and follow it to the end.

This is a pleasant, easy stroll, through a relic of the Tertiary period — the great laurel forest which covered southern Europe and North Africa some 15 million years ago. Today these flora are virtually extinct, but the Canarian archipelago harbours a few of the remaining sanctuaries. This evergreen forest is the result of climatic conditions brought about by the trade winds. At least ten species of laurel flourish here; the forest is also a refuge for ferns, fungi and lichen.

The bus ride itself brightens your day: the first thing to hit you will be the splendour of the colours — bright red poinsettias, blue morning glory, white, pink and red oleander, and the ever-present bougainvillea, with its rich hues of scarlet, orange and purple. Canary date palms give the road a touch of elegance. You'll pass through picturesque San Juan de la Rambla and then come into the pleasant sprawling town of Icod de los Vinos (known for the dragon tree shown on page 27). The ongoing route to Erjos climbs 800m/2600ft and affords some of the most splendid panoramas on the island, from intensively tilled rich pockets of volcanic soil to wild, untamed greenery, where Erjos is just a meek splash of white.

You'll be dropped off just past the CHURCH in **Erjos**. **Start out** by taking the steps alongside the church, then follow the road directly opposite the church entrance. Just over the crest, the road veers sharp right. Here keep straight ahead downhill on a path, to cross a ravine (ignore a fork to the right and, on the ascent, a fork to the left). You circle to the right of an unfinished enclosure, then climb the hillside above it, passing a faint fork off to the right. Around 10 minutes up, you're out on the forestry track signposted to 'LAS MORADAS', which you will follow all the way to the El Palmar Valley, over two hours away. Two springs en route will provide refuelling stops.

A couple of minutes along the track you're overlooking a cauldron of valleys (Picnic 17). Beyond the FIRST SPRING, you pass a path off right signposted to Las Moradas. Beyond the SECOND SPRING, you come into another, equally impressive basin and pass a track off right signposted to Las Moradas (**1h40min**). *(If you're doing either of the Alternative walks, turn right here; this track is also used in Walk 21.)* Within the next 30 minutes, just before entering the El Palmar Valley, you pass a track descending to the right, where Walk 21 joins, before heading towards Erjos. (El Palmar can also be reached via this track, as in Shorter walk 21.) Not far past the Erjos/El Palmar turn-off, you come into the **El Palmar Valley** (**2h20min**). You'll be struck by the absence of trees: the entire basin is terraced, from top to bottom, right to left. El Palmar lies almost immediately below and, much further down on the plain, Buenavista sits surrounded by banana palms.

Some 25 minutes after coming into the valley (**2h 45min**), leave the track (just beyond a bend). The turn-off is signalled by a cairn marked '**Lancito**'; opposite is a signpost for 'LAS LAGUNETAS'. Descend the path to the right, then keep left uphill at a fork. The path threads its way through abandoned and overgrown plots. Large unruly fig trees abound and, in spring, mauve and purple *Senecio* (see page 56) bloom along the route. Just over 10 minutes downhill, you come into to the picturesque village of **Las Lagunetas**, passing some houses (one may have a very unfriendly, but penned-in, dog). On reaching a crossroads, turn right. This narrow road, edged with a profusion of colourful blooms, brings you into **El Palmar** (**3h25min**). Turn left on the main road (TF436): the bus stop is 100m/yds away. Or, if you're still full of energy, use the map to follow the old, partially overgrown, stone-paved track to Buenavista, 40 minutes away.

18 RESTAURANTE FLEYTAS • MONTAÑA JALA • LOS BOLICOS • DEGOLLADA DE LA MESA • RESTAURANTE FLEYTAS

See map pages 90-91   **Distance:** 12.2km/7.6mi; 4h20min

Grade: moderate, with overall ascents/descents of 550m/1800ft. The ascent to the peak beyond the Degollada de la Mesa requires a little scrambling; some people will find it vertiginous. The weather can be very changeable; you can be engulfed in cloud within minutes.

Equipment: hiking boots, sunhat, suncream, rain-/windproof, fleece, picnic, water

How to get there and return: 🚌 325 from Puerto to/from Restaurante Fleytas, above Erjos (Timetable 16; journey time 1h15min), or by 🚗. Alternative return buses are 460 and 360 (the latter via La Montañeta).

Short walk: Restaurante Fleytas — Los Bolicos — Restaurante Fleytas: 8.2km/5.1mi; 2h25min. Quite easy, with overall ascents/descents of about 300m/1000ft; equipment and access as above. Follow the main walk, but omit the two ascents to the peaks.

Alternative walk: Puerto de Erjos — Montaña Jala — La Tabaiba — Teno Alto — Buenavista: 18km/11.2mi; 6h. *Only recommended for experienced, adventurous hikers**, on account of the very steep (700m/ 2300ft) and vertiginous descent from Teno Alto; equipment and access as main walk (🚌 325); return from Buenavista on 🚌 363 to Puerto (Timetable 6); journey time 1h20min. Alight from the bus at Puerto de Erjos, at the junction with the road to Montaña Jala. Follow the road to the summit (35min). Descend the same way for 10min, then fork left on a track (ignore the track striking off right immediately into the turn-off). Within the next 10min, just past a track forking off to the right, bear left on a path. A couple of minutes later, at a junction of paths (Cruce de Jala), descend to the right. At the fork, both branches lead down to the derelict hamlet of Los Bolicos (1h05min). Leave the hamlet on the track to the left of it; it soon becomes a path. Within 5min, fork left to a viewpoint. Then return to the junction and go left. Remain on this ridge (Cumbre de Masca, then Cumbre del Carrizal), keeping straight ahead at the only junction encountered, until you cross the TF436 at the pass of La Tabaiba (2h10min). Here pick up Walk 19 (page 98; map pages 100-101), to continue up the *cumbre*.

*If you are not sure-footed, or you suffer from vertigo, from Teno Alto use the map for Walk 20 on pages 100-101 to go from Teno Alto to La Montañeta (1h15min) and return from there on 🚌 366 to Buenavista (Timetable 11); journey time 15min, then change to 🚌 363 for Puerto (Timetable 6); journey time 1h20min.

The few ponds encountered (Tenerife's 'Lake District'!) set this walk apart from the others. Beyond them, after enjoying a stupendous view from the highest point in the western corner of the island, we follow a jungle-like trail, dripping with moss, before scrambling up to a lesser peak, even more exhilarating than the first.

Start out at **Restaurante Fleytas**, the bus stop above Erjos. Walk back down the road towards Erjos for 100m/ yds, then fork left on a track, down to the valley floor. Here you'll see several lovely ponds — if there has been adequate rainfall! Montaña Jala — your destination — is the highest point just behind the hill in the foreground. Down by the ponds, you come to a T-junction. Turn right here and, 100m/yds further on, take the track forking off to the left. It will take you up to the ridge over on the right.

Luxuriant vegetation greets you. The whole basin (Picnic 18a) is wild and unkempt, and many of the terraced plots are overgrown. Just past two ponds, you pass through a staggered junction. Follow the main track, which curves first to the right, then veers left. *But ignore a wide cairn-marked track to the left just below you at this point.* As your track ascends, ignore any farm tracks forking off to the left or right. About 10 minutes up from the basin there may be a chain across the track; if so, just walk past it. Keep straight uphill; in five minutes you're on the crest of the ridge, with a magnificent view of El Teide and a good outlook over the ponds below. A minute later, at a junction of paths to the left, keep right (**30min**; CAIRN), rounding the hillside and entering the woods. Cool, fresh, and laden with moss, your path provides a pleasant interlude on hot days. Ignore all descending paths. A little over 10 minutes along, at a junction, ascend to the left on a lesser path. *(But for the Short walk, continue straight ahead round the hillside and pick up the notes again at the 1h30min-point.)* Immediately over a small crest, veer right to cross a small *barranco,* then ignore a path to the left. Several minutes later, meet a forestry track (CAIRN) and turn left uphill *(note the lay-by here — also with a CAIRN — to relocate the path on your return).*

As the track bends to the right, rise up a small earthen bank on the left (opposite a small brown metal gate), to join the forestry road to the summit. Follow the road for just over 10 minutes, up to the antennae and fire-watch tower on **Montaña Jala** (**1h10min**). What a view! You look straight down on the cataclysm of ravines that carve up this western massif. To the south, hundreds of greenhouses sparkle under the sun. Santiago del Teide is the small settlement in the shallow valley below on the left.

Moving on, you return to the laurel forest … the best part of which is still to come. Retrace your steps back down the road and then the track. By the lay-by, pick up your ascending path and return to the JUNCTION (**1h 30min**). *(The Short walk rejoins here.)* Turn left and, a minute along, come to a fork. Head down to the right, to a beautiful spot, where the trees and rocks are cloaked in thick moss and a spring sits below a wall of basalt.

Return to the fork and turn right, to ascend to the top

of the ridge. Stay on the right-hand side of the 'clearing'. Ignore the faint fork off to the left here; keep round the edge of the valley on the sometimes-overgrown path. (Should this path become impassable, you will have to retrace your steps and use the map to follow the track to Cumbre de Bolicos.) Ten minutes from the spring you meet a wider path and turn left. At the intersection a couple of minutes uphill, turn right downhill (CAIRN). Ten minutes later you come into the derelict hamlet of **Los Bolicos** (**2h30min**), sheltering in a hollow on the ridge. This is a good place to see the bright red and yellow parasitic plant, *Cytinus hypocistis,* which resembles a fungus.

From here you ascend to the right of Montaña Jala, to the pointed rocky peak on your left. Walk back up to the path and track on the right (signposted 'PUERTO DE ERJOS') and climb the hillside (the path and track rejoin). The path veers left and rounds a narrow valley that winds its way seaward. Ignore a turn-off to the left. Twenty minutes up, you're at the **Degollada de la Mesa** (**2h55min**), with the peak just to the right. *(If you're doing the Short walk, keep straight on over this pass; see last paragraph.)*

Poke around in the bushes to find the path to the peak; it *does* exist and remains on the crest all the way up, waymarked with the odd green dot. A good 10 minutes gets you to the top, surrounded by sheer drops and enjoying a superb view into the valley of Masca below.

Back at the pass, descend a slope lightly wooded in pines. When you reach the forestry track, follow it for a little over 20 minutes, up to the road that ascends to Montaña Jala. Turn right here. Within 15 minutes, just before the TF82, turn left on a path marked by a cairn and a sign, 'EL PELADO'), descending back to the ponds. Less than 10 minutes down, you meet your outgoing path at a junction and turn right, back up to **Restaurante Fleytas** (**4h20min**) and the nearby bus stop.

The ponds above Erjos

19 LA TABAIBA • TENO ALTO • BUENAVISTA

See also photograph page 1   **Distance:** 10.5km/6.5mi; 3h30min
Grade: moderate-strenuous, with an ascent of 200m/650ft and a steep, rocky desent of 600m/1970ft. You must be sure-footed and have a head for heights (danger of vertigo); *the descent is only recommended for very experienced hikers* (otherwise, do the Alternative walk below — or consider doing the main walk in reverse: climbing is always less vertiginous than descending). *The walk is only suitable in fine weather.*
Equipment: hiking boots, warm fleece, sunhat, rain-/windproof, suncream, picnic, water
How to get there: 🚌 363 from Puerto to Buenavista (Timetable 6); journey time 1h20min; *change to* 🚌 355 to the pass of La Tabaiba (Santiago bus, *not in the timetables*; departs 09.30 *only*, Mon-Fri) — or take a taxi (5km). Since bus and taxi drivers do not know the pass by this name, and there is *no* signposting, ask for the '*mirador* above (poor en-**see**-mah day) Las Portelas'. It's the highest point on the road to Masca, and there is a large parking bay.
To return: 🚌 363 from Buenavista to Puerto (Timetable 6); journey time 1h20min

Alternative walk: La Tabaiba — Teno Alto — La Montañeta: 8.5km/ 5.3mi; 2h40min. Moderate; equipment and access as above; return on 🚌 366 to Buenavista (Timetable 11); journey time 15min; *change to* 🚌 363 to Puerto (as above). Follow the main walk to Teno Alto, then use the map for Walk 20 to reach La Montañeta (the first part of Walk 20, but in reverse). *Note:* the initial 5min descent back into the El Palmar valley is very steep and slippery; use the road if this looks too difficult.

Spectacular, exhilarating and, in places, hair-raising … but if you are sure-footed and not affected by vertigo, I highly recommend this hike. The final descent has to be one of the most impressive in the archipelago! This hike dissects the hills of Teno: rocky ridges offering stunning views, plunging gulleys, lush meadows, goatherds, and a hair-raising descent on an incredible path! Don't miss it!

Alight from the bus or taxi at the pass of **La Tabaiba** (see above). **Start out** by following the path off the parking bay, heading north. There is a superb view over the verdant cultivation in the El Palmar Valley on the right; to the left, you look across sheer plunging ravines. Your route heads up the **Cumbres de Baracán** (Picnic 19a), towards Montaña Baracán, the highest point; later, it will swing across to the left, to enter the heights of Teno. The zigzag path is clear, and *sendero turístico* signs appear at regular intervals. The slopes are a tapestry of wild flowers in spring, and goat bells tinkle in the valleys below. Los Carrizales is the small village far below to the left.

You pass a path (**30min**) ascending to **Montaña Baracán**. As the view from its summit has little more to offer, continue to the left. On reaching the top of the ridge, you look straight out over a dissected tableland. Teno Alto is the tight cluster of houses sheltering at the foot of a hill below you. Other scattered dwellings sprinkle the tops of ridges. The banana plantations of Buenavista appear through the walls of a *barranco* and, behind you, the massive shoulders of El Teide rise spectacularly.

Crossing over the ridge, you head into scrub, stride across grassy slopes, and then dip into a beautiful wood of heather. Below the wood you come to the edge of La Siete. Before entering the hamlet, turn left on a track — to a wide hillside 'balcony' with a stupendous view: a landscape of razor-sharp ridges. A little further on, turn right on a path — to an even better viewpoint, over-looking a tilting plateau of grassland with the scattered homesteads of a few goatherds. The only sound is the tinkling of goats' bells — and yappy herders' dogs. This is my favourite part of Teno; I could sit here forever … when the wind isn't blowing (Picnic 19b).

Onward bound, head back down the track to the hamlet of **La Siete**, from where you follow a narrow tarred road in a short winding descent to **Teno Alto (1h25min)**. *(Those doing the Alternative walk should now use the map overleaf, to continue to La Montañeta: follow the route of Walk 20, but in reverse.)* The main walk leaves Teno on the road ascending to the left of Bar Los Baila-deros (signposting: 'PUERTO MALO'). The Buenavista flats reappear, down through a deep ravine. A few minutes along, just after a track forks off to the right, turn off on a wide dirt path (probably once a track) descending to the right. This steep descent brings you back to the road at a point where the road curves to the left and a track forks off it to the right. Cross the track and ascend the ridge ahead (signpost 'PUERTO MALO'). Your path soon swings

The hillside balcony not far outside La Siete (Picnic 19b).

right, to pass between two hills: the prominent pointed one on the left is **Roque de la Cruz (1h40min)**. Here you find a cairn marked '**Las Barerras**' (and *perhaps* a signpost to 'Visititas'). Your path is the lower one to the right, which descends into the lush valley below. A patch of eroded hillside opposite catches the eye, with its breathtaking array of soft volcanic pinks, mauves, creams, and browns. *Sendero turístico* signs and small cairns keep you on route. Remains of a cobbled path come underfoot. You drop into a shallow V in the top of the crest and pass an

old WHEAT THRESHING CIRCLE (**1h45min**). Here the path appears to disappear off the cliffs ahead … and almost does!

Before the descent, enjoy the brilliant view over Buenavista and along the coast. Climbing a short way out of the dip, you find a gate, beyond which the descent path clings to a narrow ledge. Chiselled out of the sheer rock face and vertiginous from the outset, it bears the traces of former paving. As you zigzag down, be sure to *stop* to admire the views — and the surprising amount of plant life, incluing patches of rusty-red and lime-yellow lichen, *tabaiba, candelabra,* and *Aeoniums.* Closer to the *barranco* floor, the vegetation is head-high and jungle-thick. An hour down the cliff path, you enter the bed of a dry *barranco.* Swinging in and out of the *barranco,* you clamber over rocks and boulders. Finally you reach a track which takes you to the TF445 (**2h45min**). Follow the road to the right, to the BUS STATION at **Buenavista (3h30min)**.

See map pages 100-101; see also photograph page 1

Distance: 20km/12.5mi; 5h30min (add 1h for a detour to the lighthouse)

Grade: strenuous, with a total climb of 400m/1300ft and descent of 800m/2600ft. There is the additional hazard of loose stones on the final descent. Possibility of vertigo on two short-cut paths.

Equipment: walking boots, sunhat, fleece, rain-/windproof, picnic, plenty of water, swimwear; a torch is *essential* for the road tunnel (10min)

How to get there: 🚌 363 from Puerto to Buenavista (Timetable 6); journey time 1h20min; *change to* 🚌 366 to El Palmar (Timetable 11); journey time 15min; ask for 'el camino para Teno Alto'. Or take a taxi for this short trip of 5km

To return: 🚌 363 from Buenavista to Puerto (Timetable 6; as above)

The high, hidden, segmented valleys of the Teno are a must for those with stamina. This isolated severe landscape has a stark beauty, with soft colours emanating from the earth itself. Solitude and peace immediately come to mind. The hardships that these few inhabitants have chosen to face leave one admiring, perhaps even envying, their fortitude.

The walk begins just by the road to Teno Alto: take the path running alongside a low concrete-block wall on the left, where the sign reads 'TENO ALTO'. Head up between sagging stone walls. *Sendero turístico* signs will appear at regular intervals. In the first 20 minutes along this lush green path, you cross both a track and the Teno road. Closer to the pass, the path is very steep and slippery. Your view commands the entire valley.

You reach a PASS on the **Cumbres de Baracán (40min)** and enter the hidden valleys of Teno — a completely

Barranco de las Cuevas

different world, bleak and rugged. You're at about 800m/2600ft here; the highest point of this great mass is Montaña Baracán at 1003m/3290ft, not far away on the left. (For a better all-round view pop up to the road above.)

The now-shady path continues straight on over the pass, below the road. In a couple of minutes you meet the road again, on a bend: cross over the track branching off the road, to pick up the continuation of the path. A sign, 'SAN JERONIMO', reassures you. As you round the hillside, a short stretch of path may prove vertiginous for some. Around 15 minutes later, bear right along the crest and begin to descend into a valley (**1h10min**). After climbing a neatly-paved section of path on the far side of the valley, you round a bend and soon find yourselves on a concrete track above a small farm building. Follow this track for seven minutes, ignoring faint off-shoots, then take the wide cobbled path off to the right (just where the track swings left). You meet the Teno Alto road again several minutes uphill and cross it, passing a SHRINE dedicated to San Jerónimo on your right. Soon your curiosity is satisfied: you rejoin the road and head left into **Teno Alto** (**1h40min**).

To make for Teno Bajo, keep straight ahead across the junction (signposted 'PUNTA DE TENO'). You cross a slight crest and descend into another valley. Within 10 minutes you reach another crest and a junction, where there is a house with shutters on the right. Continue straight over the crest and then downhill, ignoring a track off to the right. The road now reverts to track. Barely 10 minutes down, you round a bend and come to a junction. Your way is downhill, to the right, signposted 'LA CUEVA'. A few minutes later you meet a road. Just beyond it, follow a faint path down to the left, on the edge of the **Barranco de las Cuevas**. The path becomes clearer further along. For the first stretch, stay to the left of the road, following the edge of the *barranco* downhill. A 5cm/2" diameter WATER PIPE is beside you. On reaching the road again, above a few buildings, follow it to your next turn-off: this comes up some 20m/yds below a house on a bend, just before the track veers right. (The yappy dogs here will alert you!) Here you pick up the path again, descending to the left (some people may find this stretch vertiginous). Keep following the WATER PIPE. You head down the hillside, at times quite close to the edge of the ravine. A tired rock wall is on your right, and you pass several abandoned stone buildings. Some metres/yards *before* the last

The dramatic descent to Teno Bajo

of the dwellings in the valley, fork left down another path, quickly reaching the bed of the *barranco*. Here you join a track (**2h35min**) and follow it to the left.

As you leave the ravine, go right at a fork and, soon after, go through a GATE (please leave it closed as requested). Along this part of the track, more of the coastal tongue comes into view, where dark lava shades meet the royal-blue sea. Fifteen minutes beyond the last houses, the track comes to a dead end, high above the plain. A wall of rocks here serves as a good windbreak. This is an excellent viewpoint and lunch spot: to the right, the jagged ravine cuts back into the mountainside; to the left is the subdued coastline's only landmark: the lighthouse, sitting on a promontory of black lava. Flickering below you are greenhouses for tomatoes. On clear days La Gomera is visible — its mountains rise very clearly out of the sea, and the two humps of La Palma stand out over to the right.

Your path continues behind the windbreak to a viewpoint, then veers left. Zigzag down the sheer escarpment. Loose rocks and gravel make it very slow going, so enjoy the superb descent *in pauses, not while on the move!* Your only landmark on this stretch is a small covered WATER TANK, about 25 minutes downhill. The path ends at the left of some large sheds at **Teno Bajo** (**3h35min**). Opposite is an enormous farm. From here it's an easy hour's stroll to the lighthouse *(faro)* and back. Then you follow the TF445 east, enjoying spectacular coastal scenery. A torch is *essential* for the tunnels. Some 50 minutes along, you pass Punta del Fraile, from where there are magnificent views out over the banana groves surrounding Buenavista. Once in **Buenavista**, keep ahead past Plaza San Sebastián, to reach the BUS STATION (**5h30min**).

21 LOS SILOS • TALAVERA • (GALERIA LAS MORADAS) • LOS SILOS

See map pages 90-91   **Distance:** 11.5km/7mi; 5h15min

Grade: very strenuous, with ascents/descents of 850m/2790ft overall. Add 200m/650ft of descent and reascent (1h) for the detour to the Galería Las Moradas. You must be sure-footed and have a head for heights (possibility of vertigo). *Only suitable in fine settled weather.*

Equipment: walking boots, sunhat, warm fleece, rain-/windproof, suncream, picnic, plenty of water

How to get there and return: 🚐 363 from Puerto to/from Los Silos (Timetable 6); journey time 1h15min, or 🚗

Short walk: Los Silos — Talavera — El Palmar: 6km/3.7mi; 2h35min. Strenuous, with a steep ascent of 700m/2300ft; equipment and access as above; return to Buenavista on 🚐 366 (Timetable 11), then 🚐 363 as above. Follow the main walk to the turn-off for Horno (2h05min), then refer to the map to descend right to El Palmar (eventually joining the end of Walk 17). When you reach the TF436 at El Palmar, the bus stop is 100m/yds to the left.

High in the hills behind Los Silos we come upon abandoned hamlets and small groves of pines. If you have the energy, be sure to take the detour to the *galería* in Las Moradas — a ravine with gushing water, hidden deep in the hills, the likes of which you won't find anywhere else on Tenerife. And on the return we follow stretches of a centuries-old manicured path. This walk is tough but, if you allow a whole day, it's manageable.

Get off the bus by the CHURCH in **Los Silos**, at the junction of Calle Susana and the bypass road. **Start out** by continuing west along the bypass road for a couple of minutes, then turn left on a road signposted 'PINA/TALAVERA'. The hike takes you up the valley ahead, mostly along the right-hand wall. Ascending past banana and citrus groves, you cross a *barranco* (**10min**) and then take a path climbing to the right — making for a chapel on the hillside above. The hillside is matted with *tabaiba,* asphodels, lavender, prickly pear, *verode, lengua de gato,* and *Aeoniums.*

Within the next 10 minutes you pass the CHAPEL, set on an (enclosed) CANAL. Thick-armed *candelabra* begin appearing, and the path is splashed with purple-flowering *Vitrium.* Los Silos lies below at the foot of a volcanic mound, swallowed up by banana groves. Closer to Talavera, you come into the pine zone, and the sheer-sided valley below closes into a narrow defile. Tierra del Trigo is the village set high in the hills two barrancos away.

Mounting a bouldery crest, you come upon the sad remains of a crumbled hamlet — **Talavera** (**1h25min**).

This pretty spot looks out over pine groves. In spring the top of the crest is carpeted in flowers. Leaving the hamlet, keep it to your right, then bear right, to ascend the ridge behind the hamlet. Now you're in cloud territory, on the edge of the laurel forest. Cushions of moss coat the rocks. Some 25 minutes above Talavera, you have an unimpeded view of the El Palmar Valley, etched from top to bottom in terracing. Yellowy-brown Canary bell flowers (see page 92) flourish alongside the path here; this creeper is prolific in the forest in springtime.

Five minutes along the narrow rocky ridge, you come to a prominent upthrust of rock with a cave-like hollow in it. A steep winding descent into the El Palmar Valley follows, in the thick of the laurel woods. Not far past the big rock, ignore a turn-off to the right signposted for 'HORNO' (**2h05min**); keep left here. *(But for the Short walk, head right, and use the map to meet the route of Walk 17 and follow it into El Palmar.)*

A steep slippery ascent brings you out onto a track a good 15 minutes uphill (ignore the path forking off left just before the track). Continuing ahead, you meet the main ERJOS/EL PALMAR TRACK (**2h30min**) cutting across your way, and you follow it to the left for the next 20 minutes.

Just before leaving the valley, you come to your turn-off on the left — a track signposted for 'LAS MORADAS' (**2h 55min**). There is usually a barrier across this track. On the descent, there is a good view back, across to the ridge you ascended. Twenty-five minutes down the track, keep an eye out for your turn-off path; it comes up just beyond a bend, and is signposted to 'LAS MORADAS' (**3h25min**). A brief steep descent follows, before the path veers left round the hillside. (Ignore the faint fork off to the right barely two minutes downhill.)

A few minutes downhill, you come to the TURN-OFF TO THE GALERIA LAS MORADAS (**3h30min**; see notes about *galerías* on pages 44-45). This will cost you close on an hour; the path is vertiginous and ranges from slightly to very overgrown (you may have to crouch down through a 'tunnel' of brambles), but still clear. If you've got the energy, it's worth seeing. The path descends to the right, and goes all the way down to the Galería Las Moradas in the Barranco de Cochinos. Ignore the path ascending to the right about halfway down.

The main walk passes by the *galería* turn-off, keeping straight ahead. This path will take you all the way back to Los Silos; there are no turn-offs. You follow some magnificent sections of old path (see opposite), and the scenery is tremendous. You pass a lone ruin some 30 minutes down, where a rocky outcrop provides the perfect viewpoint. Not long after, you pass another derelict outpost. Now descending the **Barranco de Bucarón**, the path eventually meets a concrete lane on the outskirts of **Los Silos** (**5h05min**). A few minutes down the lane, a road cuts in front of you. Turn left, quickly reaching the bypass road at its junction with Calle Susana. The BUS STOP is just here, by the CHURCH (**5h15min**).

Some 30 minutes below the turn-off to the Galería Las Moradas, you pass a lone ruin where a rocky outcrop provides the perfect viewpoint down over the banana plantations of Los Silos.

22 THE CANAL WALK: PUNTA DEL HIDALGO • BATAN DE ABAJO • BEJIA • PUNTA DEL HIDALGO

Map on reverse of fold-out touring map **Distance:** 13km/8mi; 5h

Grade: strenuous, with a steep ascent of 600m/1970ft. *Recommended for experienced and adventurous hikers only:* you must be sure-footed and have a head for heights; there are several vertiginous stretches. See photograph opposite: much of walk follows watercourses running along sheer-sided escarpments (the channels are about 45cm/18" wide and built up 30-50cm/12-20" at the sides). *The walk should only be attempted in very dry conditions, in stable weather.* **The empty channels are lethal when coated with rain-slick.**

Equipment: walking boots, sunhat, suncream, light fleece, rain-/ windproof, picnic, plenty of water; a *torch* is helpful for the longest tunnel, which has a projection at head height in the middle!

How to get there and return: 🚌 102 from Puerto to/from La Laguna (Timetable 1); journey time 45min; *change to* 🚌 105 to/from Punta del Hidalgo (Timetable 13); journey time 40min. Or 🚗: park at the *mirador*

Alternative walk: Punta del Hidalgo — Barranco del Río — Batán de Abajo — Punta del Hidalgo: distance, grade, equipment and access/ return as above. The outgoing route in the *canal* is more vertiginous than the return leg. You can avoid the worst places by following the bed of the Barranco del Río, rather than the *canal.* Follow *Walk 23* on page 111 to the log bridge, where Walk 23 crosses the Barranco del Río. Keep right here, ascending the path in the bed of the *barranco* for the next 55min, picking up the main walk again at the 1h-point.

Short walks

1 **Punta del Hidalgo — Batán de Abajo**: 6km/3.8mi; 2h30min. Grade, equipment and access as main walk (ascent of 500m/1640ft); return from Batán de Abajo to La Laguna on 🚌 074 (*not in the timetables;* Mon-Fri: 16.00, 19.50; Sat, Sun, holidays: 15.00; journey time 50min). Follow the main (or Alternative) walk to Batán de Abajo.

2 **Batán de Abajo — Bejía — Punta de Hidalgo**: 7km/4.4mi; 2h30min. Moderate, but there is a steep 15-minute descent to the *canal* (overall descent: 600m/1970ft); equipment and return as main walk; access via 🚌 074 from La Laguna to Batán de Abajo (*not in the timetables;* Mon-Fri: 07.00, 15.05; Sat, Sun and holidays: 09.05, 14.00; journey time 50min. Follow the main walk from Batán de Abajo (the 2h30min-point).

This hike is unique for its watercourses, forging their way through the wilderness. The *canal* we follow back to Punta del Hidalgo is amazing — either hacked out of the sheer rock walls of the valley or seeming to hang off them! If vertigo doesn't worry you, this thrilling, frightening hike is a 'must'. Batán, truly off the beaten track and therefore little changed by tourism, is very special. I hate to say it again but (as I say in every walk), it's my favourite village.

Leaving the **Punta del Hidalgo** bus at the last stop, you look up from the *mirador* into sheer jagged valleys that conceal magnificently-sited villages. **Start the walk** by taking the lane off to the right, immediately below the *mirador* (sign: 'Chinamada, Las Carboneras, Taganana').

Near the end of the walk, you round a bend to find an enormous rock balancing over the canal in the Barranco Seco.

A minute down, ignore a fork to the right. Two minutes later, on the very edge of the sea cliffs, just beyond the greenhouses on your right, fork right on a track (a barrier blocks the entrance to traffic). Follow this track over the *barranco* and, around five minutes uphill, turn left on a track. It takes you up to the *canal* in a minute. Turn left on the watercourse, which now becomes your way for the next 50 minutes. This is all sorts of fun. At times you're virtually crawling under rock or balancing along the edge (but do watch for places where steps cut in the rock avoid awkward passages). The ravine, with its sharp, cascading ridges and exotic plant life, constantly draws your attention: always *stop to admire the views!*

At the point where the bed of the *barranco* has almost risen to meet the *canal,* you spot a DERELICT HOUSE just up ahead (**1h**; 50min along the *canal*). Here you leave the *canal*: crossing to the left side of the *barranco*, you join the path that ascends the valley floor. A minute along, you cross the *canal* at its SOURCE; then you recross the *barranco* and ascend the nose of a rocky ridge (100m/yds past the derelict house, by a CAIRN on the right). An 'alpine' path now becomes your way: carved out of the rock, it seems at times to hang in mid air. Higher up the valley you find vineyards terracing the sheer hillsides.

Meeting a junction signposted 'PUNTA HIDALGO', around 50 minutes up from the floor of the *barranco*, bear left. Just after, your way swings left across terraced vineyards. A good five minutes further up, a spectacular view awaits you: mounting a ridge (Picnic 22), you look out over an immense valley sprinkled with little white houses tucked away in the sheer escarpments. In the background is the island's forested backbone, the *cumbre*. Here you turn right.

A couple of minutes later, you round a bend ... to see Batán straight ahead — only a crest away. This small huddle of houses clings to the nose of the ridge above a terraced hillside. It's love at first sight! Keep round the hillside to the village. Ignore all the paths turning off to plots. The dogs announce your arrival in **Batán de Abajo** (**2h30min**). The village square and a friendly bar (closed Wed) are down to the left. Don't miss the view from the square.

Then, making for Bejía, head straight up the steps from the square. A few minutes up, turn right (by a large WATER TAP and PICNIC TABLES). Your path climbs straight up and over the ridge. Chinamada (Walk 23) is a few houses snuggled into the top of the ridge on the far right. A couple of rooftops introduce Bejía, still a ridge away. Passing over the crest, ignore paths off to the left and right. You head along a cultivated shelf high on a sheer *barranco* wall … another vertiginous stretch of path.

Twenty minutes from Batán you meet a ROAD and follow it to the right, passing **Bejía** (**2h55min**) — just a few houses set amidst terraced garden plots on a rocky ridge. Less than 25 minutes downhill, the road ends. A house is below. Descend the track at the left of the house; when the track ends, take the path off to the left, down into the *barranco* below. There's no waymarking, but the steep rocky path is clear. Yet another vertiginous descent takes you down to this *barranco* bed, sometimes on all fours.

A good 15 minutes down, across the valley floor, your next *canal* awaits you, where it takes its SOURCE in the **Barranco Seco** (**3h35min**). Minutes along, just after a bend, the path leaves the *canal,* re-entering it just before it disappears into a 2 minute-long tunnel. From here on, you'll be in awe at what you see; this watercourse is a spectacular piece of engineering, balancing at the edge of the escarpment. It certainly kept *my* adrenaline flowing!

Around 30 minutes along this *canal,* you round a bend to find an enormous rock balancing at the end of the ridge (see photograph page 109). It's quite a picture. The *canal* takes you straight through it. Not long after, goats' bells alert you to civilisation. The *canal* deteriorates and finally disappears under earth. Continue on a goats' path round the valley wall (keeping to the contours at any forks) and crossing a tributary several minutes along. (Ignore the path forking off left here.) Shortly after, you come onto a track. The track soon becomes a tarred road and leads you down to **Punta del Hidalgo** (**5h**). At a junction, go straight ahead. (But motorists should turn right here; this road goes straight back to the *mirador.*) You meet the TF13 just to the right of the CHURCH, where your bus stops.

23 PUNTA DEL HIDALGO • CHINAMADA • LAS CARBONERAS

Photograph: the Barranco del Río, below the twin peaks of the Roque Dos Hermanos

Map on reverse of the fold-out touring map

Distance: 7km/4.3mi; 2h 45min (plus optional detour of 25min to the Mirador Era de las Almácigas)

Grade: strenuous climb (700m/2300ft overall); possibility of vertigo

Equipment: walking boots, fleece, rain-/windproof, sunhat, picnic, water

How to get there: 🚌 102 from Puerto to La Laguna (Timetable 1); journey time 45min; *change to* 🚌 105 to Punta del Hidalgo (Timetable 13); journey time 40min

To return: 🚌 075 from Las Carboneras to La Laguna (Timetable 17); journey time 1h05min; *change to* 🚌 102 to Puerto (as above)

Alternative walk: Las Carboneras — Chinamada — Las Carboneras: 6km/3.7mi; 2h. Easy-moderate, with ups and downs of about 300m/1000ft. Access as for Walk 24, page 114; return by the same bus. From the bus stop, walk back out of Las Carboneras for four minutes. Then, after the road bends to the left, ascend a path to the right (which *may be* signposted 'LAS ESCA-LERAS'). You'll pass a *fuente* (spring) and then come to the Escaleras *mirador*, at a junction (25min; Picnic 23b). Keep right at the junction. When the path forks, head uphill to the right. The path rounds a house around 10 minutes up from the junction; ignore the path descending to the left here. Approaching Chinamada, ignore a faint path striking off to the right. Minutes later, on reaching the road (1h15min), turn right for Las Carboneras, 45min away — or, before doing so, visit the Mirador Era de las Almácigas, a 25-minute detour (see the notes for the main walk at the 2h-point).

O ur starting point, Punta del Hidalgo, sits at the end of a steep ridge running down to the coast from the heights of the Anaga range. Get off the bus at the *mirador* just past the village, above the mouth of Barranco del Río. The valley looks impassable from here, as it rises steeply into sharp-edged ridges. Playa de los Troches (Picnic 23a), a rocky beach, is partially hidden by the cliffs below. All this comes as an abrupt change from the market garden plains of La Laguna and the rolling meadows of Tegueste, a wide, sloping valley passed on our descent to Punta del Hidalgo. Chinamada, a tiny, sprinkled hamlet, will delight you with its cave dwellings.

Start the walk at the *mirador*. Follow the concrete lane below the viewpoint down to the right (signposted 'CHI-NAMADA' and 'LAS CARBONERAS'). In a couple of minutes, with the beach falling away below you on the left, you pass large greenhouses. The surface changes to gravel underfoot. Continue straight downhill. Soon the track ends, just before a rocky promontory. Continue down a concrete lane behind a chain barrier, descending steeply into the *barranco*. The twin peaks of the Roque Dos Hermanos (Two Brothers; see photograph page 111) rise up ahead. Typical coastal, salt-resistant vegetation accompanies you: *tabaiba, verode* and *Aeoniums*. The lane passes a derelict building and, just after, you cross a small log footbridge over a dry stream bed at the mouth of the Barranco del Río. Over the stream, you begin ascending this *barranco* on a path cut into the embankment.

Above the *barranco* you skirt a thick stone wall. As you begin your (sometimes vertiginous) ascent, great arms of *cardón,* growing out of the slope, will leave you astonished at their size. Purple flowers enrich the setting too — especially the sea lavender (see page 56), which begins flowering in January. Caves of varying sizes and shapes scar the ridge. Forty minutes up, take care to keep left at a faint fork off to the right (a green arrow and dots alert you to your route). A further 20 minutes up, you come to a look-out point with superb views towards sharp, abrupt ridges dropping down to the sea. More fine views follow, as the path briefly makes its way along the edge of the cliffs, where you will hear and see birds darting about. Then, once again, you head back into the valley.

Soon you will notice a distinct change in the vegetation. *Asphodelus,* with its long, thin green leaves and flowers, covers the slope, with the help of grass. A few terraced plots dig back into the inclines. A grassy hill, hanging off the top of a ridge, marks a good spot for surveying the valley below and the banana palms engulfing Punta del Hidalgo. From here on, the way

Chinamada: like the Guanches, many of these country folk have made their homes in caves nestled in the rocky faces of the ridge.

becomes steeper, with steps cut into the edge of the ridge.

A kingdom of sheer, narrow valleys segments the range. Farmers have terraced the slightest ease in the mountainsides, from the summits down. On rounding a bend, neat stepped plots announce the beginnings of Chinamada. You'll probably reach for your camera at once, to capture on film the houses snuggled into the mountainside. Stone-terraced gardens sit below them. Just beyond these dwellings, you meet a road behind the PLAZA in **Chinamada (2h)**. There is a bar here, but it is closed Mon/Tue.

(The 25 minute detour to the Mirador Era de las Almácigas leaves from behind this plaza. Climbing above an inhabited cave dwelling, the path circles the left wall of this enclosed valley, where strips of terracing cascade down the hillsides. Further on, you pass a row of abandoned caves and ascend a ridge. Ten minutes from the plaza, you round the hillside to descend to the *mirador* — a balcony hanging over precipitous cliffs, from where you have a spectacular view of the island plunging into the sea and over to Punta del Hidalgo in the west.)

The main walk makes straight for Las Carboneras, following the road all the way. Beyond Chinamada's plaza, fresh meadows, full of clover, roll off the slopes. The mountaintops in front of you are now covered in trees and heather. Heading out of the village, you spot the lovely little white house shown opposite, protruding out of the side of the ridge on your left. A minute further uphill, another house lies over to the right. (The Alternative walk descends the driveway of this latter house.) Climbing out of the valley, you pass a basic picnic site with tables and benches by the side of the road.

Fifteen minutes uphill, the road cuts through a ridge, affording a spectacular view as you cross another crest. The long deep Barranco de Taborno runs far below. A finely-etched ridge rises up from this valley, leaving only the highest elevations of the Anaga in view. The Roque de Taborno (Walk 24) thrusts its peak above the rest of this razor-edge, while Taborno itself, a handful of white dwellings, straddles the crest midway along.

From the viewpoint follow the road for another 25 minutes, before coming into **Las Carboneras (2h45min)**, an attractive mixture of old and new houses, resting on a cultivated hillock extending into the valley. The BUS STOP is at the village entrance, by the CHURCH.

24 LAS CARBONERAS • TABORNO • ROQUE DE TABORNO • CASA CARLOS

Map: reverse of fold-out touring map; see also photos pages 23, 30, 126
Distance: 8km/5mi; 3h25min

Grade: strenuous, with ascents totalling about 600m/2000ft; *the main walk is recommended for experienced, adventurous walkers only* (see also Alternative walk); danger of vertigo along the ridge beyond Taborno.

Equipment: walking boots, fleece, rain-/windproof, sunhat, whistle, water, picnic (or have a meal at Casa Carlos)

How to get there: 🚌 102 from Puerto to La Laguna (Timetable 1); journey time 45min; *change to* 🚌 075 to Las Carboneras (Timetable 17); journey time 40 minutes. Or 🚗, in combination with Timetable 17 or returning to it via the road from Taborno (the 2h20min point).
To return: same buses

Alternative walk: Las Carboneras — base of Roque de Taborno — Las Carboneras: 7km/4.3mi; 3h. Grade as above, but without the vertiginous and potentially dangerous circuit of the rock. Access/return, equipment as above. Follow the main walk for 1h30min, then return to the 1h20min-point in the walk. From there pick up the main walk again at the 2h10min-mark, to reach Casa Carlos.

We enjoy our first view of Roque de Taborno when the bus emerges from the wooded slopes on its descent to Las Carboneras. This perfectly-shaped 'spike' (see page 30) is a prominent feature of the Anaga's landscape of razor-sharp crests. Our hike circles the base of this great sculpture. From the north side of the rock, a wealth of coastal scenery lies before us. The small pockets of fertile, stepped slopes sitting far out of reach give us some idea of how valuable this arable land once was.

Start out at the bus stop in **Las Carboneras**. Head back out of the village, the way the bus came, for 150m/yds. Then leave the road opposite the BAR VALENTIN, taking the tarred lane heading down into the *barranco* on your left. After 70m/yds, just below house No 2, turn right down concrete steps signposted 'TABORNO'. Now a partly overgrown, but still clear path takes you down grassy slopes. Ignore two paths off to the left and round the hillside, always remaining on the widest path, since many paths branch off to plots. Around 25 minutes downhill, you cross the stream bed in the **Barranco de Taborno**. Now, on the very steep ascent up the other side, ignore any side-paths. On coming to some fields (**45min**), ignore a turn-off to the right. When you reach the TF138 (**50min**), turn left and follow it into **Taborno** (**1h**). The square rises strategically atop the high thin ridge partitioning the Barranco de Taborno and the Barranco Afur de Tamadite. This widely-dispersed village could undoubtedly claim to have the best views on the island.

Facing the small CHAPEL in the square, head up the ramp at the right of it. Half a minute up, veer right. Three minutes along, when the lane forks, bear right (don't go up the steps). All the houses here are tiny and well glued to the top of the ridge. Little gardens hug their bases, and prickly pear and aloes surround the lot. Follow the now-narrower lane until it forks (at the bottom of some steps). The walk will continue to the left, down through a small open copse. But before heading on, don't miss the *mirador* down to the right, with its excellent views down into the Afur Valley and the tucked-away village of Afur (Walk 25; photograph page 119). Then head down through the copse on concrete steps. At the next fork (just after crossing a narrow ridge of rock), swing right on an earthen path. Head towards a SMALL HOUSE and pass above it (**1h20min**). On rounding the nose of a ridge, you enjoy superb views: Playa del Tamadite is seen at the mouth of the *barranco* far below on your right, and the two Roques de Anaga sit off the shore. Just after the viewpoint you pass through a GATE, closing it behind you.

Soon the ridge narrows, and you continue along the crest. The walls of the Barranco de Taborno, 'veined' with dykes, are quite spectacular from here. Horizontal strips of smooth green mark the patches of cultivation along the slopes of the ridge. Three minutes along this neck of land, the path forks: head left uphill. On reaching the TOP OF THE RIDGE (**1h30min**; Picnic 24), enjoy the view, then turn right and continue around the side of the slope. A minute along, you pass below a small STONE HUT/GOAT PEN, built into the rock on the crest above. You are now near the base of the rock, which looks less impressive from this angle. *(The Alternative walk turns back here.)*

To begin circling the **Roque de Taborno**, head down to the left. No turn-offs are necessary, so ignore the paths off to the left some minutes along. After about 10 minutes' walking round the rock (just past a small rock slide and round the end of a small ridge), the route changes abruptly. Don't continue past the plots ahead: climb steeply up the ridge just to the right. Your target is the rock: head up to it, over rocks and along goats' paths (PINK DOT WAYMARKS). On nearing the rock, continue round to the left (those who suffer from vertigo may find this stretch unnerving). Ahead, razor-sharp peaks along the coastline fall into the sea, and Almáciga (Walk 28; photograph page 22) is a cluster of white, lost in the upheaval of pinnacles to the east. As you continue round, directly beneath the rock, the beautiful

Afur Valley opens up. Further along, you come to the remains of another GOATS' PEN. Cross through it, to pick up the path — which seems to disappears off the hillside. *Cautiously* make your way round the side of the rock; this vertiginous stretch takes about half a minute. This goats' path leads you back to the first goats' pen you passed, but now *above* it. Here you clamber down to your original path and retrace your steps to the HOUSE first met at the 1h20min-point (**2h10min**). Just past this house, climb down the right-hand side of the ridge and join a path below, high up in the precipitous, winding Barranco de Taborno. Always keep left and uphill, back to the centre of **Taborno** (**2h20min**).

Leaving Taborno, ascend the stone ramp on the left signposted 'CRUZ DEL CARMEN' (two minutes out of the village, just past the electricity transformer building). This path takes you up to the crest of the ridge. After 15 minutes you meet the outward route of Walk 25. Stay on the top of this ridge (*always keeping to the widest, clearest path*) and huff and puff your way up to **Casa Carlos** (**3h25min**). The BUS STOP is at the junction two minutes up the road.

After rounding the Roque de Taborno for about 10 minutes, you climb steeply up to the right — to enjoy this magnificent view.

25 CASA CARLOS • AFUR • PLAYA DEL TAMA-DITE • AFUR • ROQUE NEGRO • TF12

Map on reverse of the fold-out touring map; see also photographs pages 2, 23, 125

Distance: 14km/8.7mi; 6h

Grade: very strenuous descent of 900m/3000ft and ascent of 800m/2600ft; possibility of vertigo; *recommended for experienced hikers only*

Equipment: walking boots, sunhat, fleece, rain-/windproof, whistle, picnic, water

How to get there: 🚌 102 from Puerto to La Laguna (Timetable 1); journey time 45min; *change to* 🚌 075 to Casa Carlos (Timetable 17); journey time 25min. Or by 🚗 in combination with Timetable 18

To return: 🚌 76 from Roque Negro to La Laguna (Timetable 18); journey time about 50min, or 🚌 077 from the Roque Negro turn-off to La Laguna (Timetable 19); journey time 45min; *change to* 🚌 102 to Puerto (as above)

Short walks

1 Casa Carlos — Taborno — Casa Carlos: 7km/4.3mi; 2h15min. Moderate descent/ascent of 400m/1300ft. Equipment and access as above; return on the same bus (or 🚗 to/from Casa Carlos). Follow the main walk for 50min; then, instead of going right, head left and follow the road to Taborno. At Taborno pick up Walk 24 at the 2h20min-point (page 116), to get back to Casa Carlos.

2 Afur — Playa del Tamadite — Taganana: 7.4km/4.6mi; 2h30min. Moderate descent/ascent of 250m/820ft, with some stretches of vertiginous path; equipment as main walk; access on 🚌 102 (as above); *change to* 🚌 076 for Afur (Timetable 18); journey time 1h; return on 🚌 246 from Taganana (Timetable 14); journey time 45min. Follow the main walk from Afur (the 1h30min-point) to Playa del Tamadite (1h). *Don't swim here!* To continue to Taganana, head back to the last stream crossing, a minute back, and ascend the path off left that climbs above a big rock. This path takes you all the way to Taganana without any turn-offs. You pass below a farm shed built into a large boulder (35min) and reach a spectacular viewpoint (50min), where you join a track. Remain on this track, passing a hamlet in 15min and ignoring a road climbing to the right a few minutes later. Then meet a road above Taganana: turn right on this road but, after 50m/yds, head left downhill on a lane between the houses. Then turn right into the village (1h30min from the beach). The bus stop is on the main road, behind the church.

W inter is often wet, but the Afur Valley is at its best then. The main stream carries enough water to hold pools big enough for a dip. Summer reduces the stream to a weary trickle, with only a few stagnant pools remaining. The days are hot then, and the landscape burns under the strong sun as the fresh green flora fade. The views on our descent open up the dim corners of this rugged landscape, and the sound of cascading water accompanies us for much of the way. Our ascent — tough as it is — is made easier by a couple of local bars, full of atmosphere!

The walk begins at **Casa Carlos**, just downhill from Cruce Las Carboneras, where you leave the bus. Take the signposted lane running downhill, on the right-hand side of the restaurant. A minute down, pass to the left of another house. Here the track becomes a wide path *(very slippery when wet)*, as it slides down the ridge. In less than five minutes ignore forks both to the left and right. A minute later, you find yourselves above a small weekend cottage secured to the top of the ridge, overlooking the Afur Valley.

At **27min** you leave this ridge and descend a path on your right (there is a telephone pole above this junction). You zigzag down the hillside, then briefly ascend to the left, to an adjoining ridge overlooking the **Barranco de Guarda**. Your route continues along the crest of the ridge, with uninterrupted vistas of Taborno and Roque Negro, the black, monumental mound of rock rising up out of the landscape on your right. A small white village of the same name nestles slightly below it.

You meet the TABORNO ROAD at **50min**. *(The Short walk keeps left here.)* Cross the road and, just below it, come to a WATER TAP on the right. Some buildings stand over to the left, and a stupendous panorama lies before you: Playa del Tamadite (your next landfall), the far ridges that rise and fall as they head seaward, and Roque Negro. From the water tap, continue down over the ridge to the right. On the descent, hamlets and solitary houses appear out of nowhere, on all sides of the valley. Two minutes down, you pass beside the cave dwellings shown on page 125. The path brushes to the left of them and falls away to the valley floor. A signposted path joins you from the right and another path joins from the left within the next 10 minutes. Soon a most beautiful sight appears — an intimate cluster of white cottages, hedged in behind prickly pear, cuddling a crest of rock. From here a wide concrete path comes underfoot. You pass just below this hamlet. Ignore a track to the left and continue downhill on concrete, then swing over to the left side of the ridge and continue on down to the stream. Afur, lodged in a swollen ridge of rock, is seen at its best from this approach.

A BRIDGE carries you across the stream at **1h30min**. After another crossing, a minute later, you climb to **Afur**, where there is a bar with the friendliest owner on the island (just past the CHAPEL). To make for the beach, follow the concrete path past the bar for for some 15m/yds, then turn right down an earthen path. When you come to the parking area, turn left on a signposted track that passes below the SCHOOL. Turn right on a path with a make-shift sign, cross the end of a track and come upon A FINGER OF ROCK at the left of the path. Starting the descent, you find yourselves not far above the **Barranco Afur de Tamadite** and small cultivated plots.

About 10 minutes from Afur, at the end of a ridge (by a LARGE BALANCING ROCK), turn sharp right and pick up another signposted path. It rises at first but, two minutes along, it descends steep gravelly rock and concrete steps. This steep descent is protected by wooden handrails (mentally reassuring for vertigo sufferers, *but don't lean*

View down over Afur from the water tap near the track to Taborno

on them!). From the next crest, another steep descent takes you down to the stream, where a dyke slices across the landscape and the *barranco*. You go through the DYKE and come to a scenic spot in the gorge, just beyond the stream crossing. From here steps take you part of the way up the rocky embankment. A good 10 minutes later, the beach comes into view. On passing through a neat terraced vineyard in another two minutes, keep right, down to the valley floor. The path now follows the stream bed all the way to **Playa del Tamadite (2h30min)**. En route you pass a couple of beautiful rock pools. The stony beach is flanked by sheer high cliffs. It's an ideal spot for solitude … except for weekends. *But swimming here is suicidal!*

The 1h30min return along the same clear path is straightforward. Back in **Afur (4h)**, head up past the CHAPEL, then descend the path on the right, just behind the tall electricity building (your outgoing path). A couple of minutes down, cross the first bridge below Afur, then turn left immediately. Continue up to the houses above, soon passing an appealing house. A couple of minutes past it, at a junction, turn right. A minute later, just above a street lamp, the path swings up left to climb the hillside. Ignore a path to the right, to two houses, then veer right above these houses, towards a TV antenna on the hillside not far ahead. You round the hillside into the **Barranco del Agua**. Ignoring faint goat paths, you now begin a noticeable ascent. Fifteen minutes uphill, from the top of a ridge, you look straight onto a sheer rock face clinging to the ridge, where the little white cave house shown on page 2 sits precariously on a thin ledge. It's quite a picture — two steps out of the front door, and you'd tumble into the gorge. From this point, head up to the right. Another path joins you from the left about eight minutes past the house, and a second one comes from the right a few minutes later.

Some 50 minutes up from Afur you pass several houses and come onto a small road which takes you up to the TF136 (**4h50min**) and the STOP FOR BUS 076 (recommended for motorists returning to Casa Carlos). The enormous 'Black Rock' for which the village is named surges up before you here. Walk on into **Roque Negro**, then continue up the road for 20-25 minutes. Just after rounding a sharp bend and passing a BUS SHELTER, climb a beautiful shady path on the left, signposted 'DEGOLLADA DE LAS HIJAS'. It leads to the main road (TF12; **6h**). The BUS STOP is 100m/yds to the right, opposite a bar/café.

26 PICO DEL INGLES • BARRANCO DE TAHODIO • SANTA CRUZ

Map on reverse of the fold-out touring map

Distance: 8km/5mi; 2h50min

Grade: easy-moderate descent of 1000m/3300ft

Equipment: walking boots, fleece, windproof, sunhat, picnic, water

How to get there: 🚌 102 from Puerto to La Laguna (Timetable 1); journey time 45min; *change to* 🚌 075, 076, 077 or 073 (Timetables 17-20); journey time 30min. Ask for 'Pico del Inglés'; the bus stops at the turn-off to this viewpoint.
To return: 🚌 245, 246, 247 or 910 on Avenida de Anaga to the bus station, then 🚌 102 from Santa Cruz to Puerto (as above)

Mirador Pico del Inglés is the magnificent starting point for this walk. From this *mirador* we look out east to the mass of valleys cutting up the Anaga Peninsula, and west to El Teide and the plains of La Laguna and La Esperanza. We also have a preview of our route immediately below on the right. The best time of year to do this walk is in winter, when small waterfalls and rock pools fill the bed of the Tahodio *barranco;* in summer the lower reaches are dry.

From the bus stop, head straight along to the *mirador* — some 10 minutes from the TF12. After enjoying the views, walk down the steps to the left of the *mirador,* above a derelict building (where you *may* see a sign, 'BARRIO DE LA ALEGRIA'). **Start the walk here:** the path is flanked by tree heather; it takes you round the back of the building. Ignore all paths off to the left.

Come to the remains of a house and a cave (**15min**). A minute later, ignore a small path to the left. Two minutes further on, passing through an intersection of three paths, keep to the middle route along the ridge. From the top of a crest (the **Cabezo del Viento**; Picnic 26) you have views down into the valleys on either side. A dark, muddy dam can be seen in the valley floor. Less than 10 minutes from the intersection, the path forks. Keep right. As you descend, parts of Santa Cruz appear and, beyond it, the inclines of La Esperanza. El Teide, the island's masterpiece, rises impressively in the background. The nose of a ridge supplies the perfect viewpoint. A little over five minutes from this viewpoint, ignore two paths striking off left, one after the other.

Around **45min** into the hike, you pass some closed-up dwellings high on the slopes (you may notice two rooms cut into the side of the embankment, before you reach the houses). Approaching another house, you encounter two turn-offs two minutes apart: go right at the first and left at the second. The path passes below the house, where you reach a junction and descend to the right (signpost: 'BARRIO DE LA ALEGRIA').

Shortly after, you cross the bed of the narrow **Barranco de Valle Luis**. Remaining on the right-hand side of this *barranco*, you pass below two more deserted houses a minute later. Skirt a very small, dry dam (**1h30min**) on the left, from which a *canal* veers off round the slope to the right. Just past the dam, ignore a path to the right: keep left, through abandoned fields. You recross the main stream twice in fairly quick succession, then pass some neat plots on your right — almond, fig and loquat trees make this a pleasant spot. One more stream crossing takes you past a farm shed, where chained dogs go beserk! The *barranco* has meanwhile narrowed quite considerably.

Cross the stream bed twice more, ignore a fork off to the left, and then meet a road (**2h05min**). Follow this road down the **Barranco de Tahodio**, all the way to the AVENIDA DE ANAGA (**2h50min**). The BUS STOP for the centre of **Santa Cruz** lies a couple of minutes along to the right.

At about 45min en route, the nose of a ridge supplies a perfect viewpoint, before you descend.

27 TAGANANA • AFUR • TABORNO • LAS CARBONERAS

Map on reverse of touring map; see also photographs pages 30, 119
Distance: 9.2km/5.7mi; 4h35min
Grade: strenuous, with steep ascents (900m/3000ft overall) and descents (500m/1650ft overall)
Equipment: walking boots, sunhat, fleece, rain-/windproof, water, picnic
How to get there: 🚌 102 from Puerto to Santa Cruz (Timetable 1); journey time 1h; *change to* 🚌 246 to Taganana (Timetable 14); journey time 45min
To return: 🚌 075 from Las Carboneras to La Laguna (Timetable 17); journey time 1h05min; *change* to 🚌 102 to Puerto (as above)
Short walks

1 Taganana — viewpoint over the Afur and Taganana valleys — Taganana: 4.5km/2.8mi; 1h40min. Strenuous ascent/descent of under 400m/1300ft; equipment and access as above; return on the same bus (or access by 🚗 to/from Taganana). Follow the main walk for 1h and return the same way.

2 Casa Forestal de Taganana — Taganana: 3.5km/2mi; 1h40min. Moderate, with a steep descent of 600m/1970ft *(dangerous if wet)*; equipment as main walk, access on 🚌 077 (Timetable 19) from La Laguna to the *casa forestal*, beyond La Cumbrilla; journey time 45min; return on 🚌 246 from Taganana to Santa Cruz (Timetable 14); journey time 40min. A track runs past the left-hand side of the forestry house: take the path forking right off this track, signposted for Taganana. A couple of minutes uphill, at a cave, ignore a fork off to the right. Minutes later, pass a turn-off to the left and begin the steep descent into the Barranco de la Iglesia. Less than 50 minutes down, leave the forest to descend amidst plots, ignoring a fork off to the right three minutes later. At 1h15min meet the Afur/Taganana junction, and descend to right. On coming to the road, bear left and, two minutes later, on a sharp bend, descend a concrete lane to the right (Camino Portugal). Rejoining the road, go right. When you reach the church in Taganana, walk to the right of it, then take the first left, to the TF134. The bus stop is opposite.

Discovering the rural depths of the Anaga involves high ascents over long lateral ridges and descents into deep, shady valleys. Here's your chance to meet the locals as they work their fields and collect fodder for their animals. Break up this rather long walk with a refueling stop at the amiable bar in Afur. It's my favourite: the owner still has time for tourists and hikers. Short walk 2 follows the magnificent old path from the *cumbre* to Taganana, a serpentine descent down the face of a sheer escarpment, in the depths of the cool, damp, moss-laden laurel wood.

Taganana is a beautiful farming village with cobbled streets and typical Canarian dwellings. Your bus stop is the second in the valley. The BUS SHELTER, where **the walk starts**, is in a parking bay. Cross the road and follow the narrow tarred road up into the village. Within a minute, ignore a lane off to the right. Turn left here and then go right immediately. In half a minute, at another junction, turn left. Here's your chance to capture some really good photos of rural life: arms of closely-knit houses extend down and across the slope. Palms, loquats, dragon trees and orange trees adorn individual gardens. After crossing a small bridge, the road continues up the hillside, but you do not. Beyond the bridge (**5min**), take the second left turn up a narrow street (CAMINO PORTUGAL) which soon becomes a wide cobbled path. A few minutes of winding up between beautiful old houses brings you onto the road again, where you head left. Two minutes up the road, turn off on a cobbled path (signposted to 'AFUR'); it skirts the right-hand side of a *barranco,* where the last houses of the village huddle together.

On coming to a fork (**25min**), go right (there *may* be a sign for 'AFUR'). The path takes you up to a track, where you turn left uphill. After 100m/yds, at a fork, keep left on a cobbled track, and after another 100m take the small flight of steps on the right, on to a donkey track. Keep straight uphill past freshly-tilled land, much of it vine-yards that produce Taganana's *vino rosado.* Higher up on the grassy slopes, the bleating of goats echoes across the hills. The path narrows, and slowly the slopes close out Taganana. The only noticeable landmark will be a sprawling mass of large boulders covered with grey lichen, running down the slope on the left.

On coming to a PASS south of the **Roque de Anima (1h)**, you overlook two very different valleys: the Taganana is a large valley, with sharp outlines and enormous salients of rock jutting out of the landscape, while the Afur Valley is a mould of ridges and gulleys. Lone dwellings perch on these ridges, above the valleys that slice up the landscape. Roque de Dentro rises out of the sea far in the back-ground, over on the Taganana side of the ridge. *(Short walk 1 turns back here.)*

To head on to Afur, keep right and downhill on an earthen path. Ignore a path turning off to the right a minute down; then ignore all further forks. Sheltered by incon-sistent patches of tree heather, this path takes you down to the first habitations, 15 minutes below the crest. Here you join a concrete lane (and may encounter an un-pleasant, but usually chained, dog). A steep 15-minute descent brings you to the road leading to Afur, where you keep right downhill, accompanied by the sounds of a babbling brook. Some 15 minutes down the road, below

This group of houses, concealed in the rock below the local 'laundry', comes as a surprise on the path between Afur and Taborno (Walks 25 and 27).

a small parking bay on the left, descend steps into the centre of **Afur** (**1h45min**) — just a church, a bar/shop, and a few modest houses.

Your continuation to Taborno is *not signposted.* It starts just behind the TALL ELECTRICITY SUBSTATION that you passed on your way down into Afur, just before the little church. Follow this path down to a confluence of streams, an ideal picnic spot. There are few places on Tenerife where the water flows so abundantly, and even this source dries to a trickle in high summer. A small concrete bridge takes you over the first stream, from where you bear right to a second stream crossing a minute later. Cascading water pours into an already-overflowing pool.

Once over the second bridge, head up the ridge; don't bear right. *Asphodelus,* with its long, thin, blade-like leaves and white-flowering stalks, covers the slope, along with scatterings of purple *Senecio.* The view back to Afur from here shows its superb setting, as the great wall of rock plays guardian to the little houses in its niches. When the path forks, just below a hamlet, keep to the left of the ridge. Rock walls, a deep mauve in colour, and untamed clumps of prickly-pear cactus prevent you from catching more than a fleeting glimpse of the individual houses. Ignore the faint fork off to the left not far above the houses (there *may* be a sign for 'TABORNO' here); then keep right all the way up.

You will be surprised to come upon yet another group of houses (photograph above). Concealed from the rest of the valley, they are set back safely into the side of the

Taborno

ridge. The path brushes past them. From above them, you have a superb outlook: the view catches all the small dwellings sheltering behind rocky ridges and in corners of the valley. Roque Negro, a solid mass of black rock rising up from the slopes and encircled by trees at its base, stands out well, slightly to your right. A minute later, by a WATER TAP on the crest, you enjoy views down to the beach. This is the local laundry spot. The two farmhouses, a little below you to the left, are the last of the solitary homes before Taborno. Make for the road above the houses and follow it to **Taborno** (**3h30min**). Red-flowering aloes cheer your approach to the large, open square, from where there are tremendous views across the razor-sharp ridges.

Las Carboneras is now just over on the next ridge. To reach the path leading to it, follow the tarred road out of Taborno for about 10 minutes. Some 150m/yds before your turn-off, there is a sign indicating the road to Las Carboneras. Your path, marked with a CAIRN, leaves the road at the *next* gap in the roadside barrier. A minute downhill, this steeply-descending path passes the remains of an old SHRINE embedded in the slope on the left, assuring you it's the correct route. Just down from the shrine, the path forks. Keep left and head towards the garden plots. The bottom of the *barranco* is where you are heading, so ignore all turn-offs.

Around 15 minutes off the road you cross a trickle of water running down the *barranco*. From here on, it's a steady climb (ignore all turn-offs) past plots and grassy slopes. On reaching the TF145, the BUS STOP is to your right, just where you enter **Las Carboneras** (**4h35min**).

28 EL BAILADERO • CHINOBRE • CABEZO DEL TEJO • EL DRAGUILLO • ROQUE DE LAS BODEGAS

Map on reverse of the fold-out touring map; see also photographs pages 22, 32-33

Distance: 10km/6.2mi; 4h20min

Grade: moderate ascent of 300m/1000ft, followed by a steep descent of 800m/2600ft

Equipment: walking boots, fleece, rain-/windproof, whistle, picnic, water

How to get there: 🚌 102 from Puerto to Santa Cruz (Timetable 1); journey time 1h; *change to* 🚌 246 (Timetable 14); journey time 45min. Leave the bus at the El Bailadero stop (just before the tunnel). Or by 🚗 in combination with Timetable 14.
To return: 🚌 246 from Roque de las Bodegas to Santa Cruz (Timetable 14); journey time 55min; *change to* 🚌 102 to Puerto (as above)

Short walks

1 Benijo — El Draguillo — Benijo: 3.5km/2.1mi; 1h15min. Easy climb of 100m/300ft; equipment as above, but stout shoes will suffice; access by 🚗 to/from Benijo. Use the map on the reverse of the touring map to reach El Draguillo by track and return the same way.

2 El Bailadero — Chinobre — Cabezo del Tejo — Chamorga: 7.5 km/4.6mi; 3h. Moderate, with an ascent of 300m/1000ft and descent of 400m/1300ft; equipment and access as main walk; return on 🚌 247 from Chamorga to Santa Cruz (Mon-Sat *only:* 16.30). Follow the main walk to the El Draguillo turn-off, then head right for Chamorga, 30min away (keep left at the junction encountered en route).

Our journey begins along the coast, as we leave the port city of Santa Cruz, and it finishes as we descend to the dramatic northern coast and its isolated villages. In between, high forested mountain trails rise and fall over moss-cushioned crests. Remains of the original laurel forests darken and roof our way. Unsurpassed views lie at regular intervals along this spine of the Anaga range.

Your bus stop is just before a road tunnel that takes the TF134 into the Taganana Valley. Although you've bought a ticket for El Bailadero, reaching this *mirador* involves a 15-minute hike. **The path begins** just across the road from the PARKING AREA/BUS STOP. Keep right at the junction under 10 minutes up. Come to the TF123 and bear right (a bar/restaurant is to the left). Follow this road for the next half hour, then watch for your path off left (**45min**), 100m/yds short of the KM2 ROAD MARKER. Climb a set of rough steps leading into trees (there may be some rudimentary hand-rails by the path). Almáciga is glimpsed far below. Go left at a fork some 10 minutes up the path. Beyond here, keep to the main path, ignoring all turn-offs downhill to the left.

On leaving the trees and meeting the road, follow it to the left downhill. A little over five minutes along you

In the laurel forest, between Chinobre and Roque de Anambra

come to the **Anaga Forestry Park** (Picnic 28a). Your turn-off, *before* the KM5 road marker, is indicated only by a rusty bus stop sign. Climb the track on your left (but *not* the track on the *far* left). Soon the track narrows to a path. After about 20 minutes, turn left to the **Chinobre** *mirador,* a rocky nodule three minutes uphill (**1h40min**). At a height of 909m/2980ft, this is one of the best viewpoints on the whole island, equalled only by Teide and Guajara. Your views encompass El Teide, Santa Cruz, San Andrés, Taganana, Taborno and Almáciga. Multitudes of ridges dissect the backbone of the Anaga into narrow isolated valleys.

Back on the main path, turn left. A minute downhill, again fork left *(don't miss this turn; watch for a tiny rusty signpost).* You're now walking in the setting shown above. A further 30 minutes brings you face-to-face with a large projection of rock towering above the trees. This bare-faced rock is called Anambra, and it makes another good viewpoint over the hidden northern valleys. **Cabezo del Tejo** (**2h20min**) is yet another magnificent lookout, with panoramas to the west.

Continue on the steeply descending path at the end of this viewpoint. On coming to an intersection with a sign for 'EL DRAGUILLO', turn left. *(But for Short walk 2, keep right.)* Once you emerge from the trees, El Draguillo discloses itself sitting back on the sea-cliffs. From here the village is a tight bunch of dulled rooftops, smothered in prickly pear (photograph pages 32-33). Forty minutes down from the junction, ignore a turn-off to the left (in front of a huge rock). At just over **3h20min** you meet the 'king' of dragon trees outside **El Draguillo**. It is, of course, for this DRAGON TREE that the village was named. But 'El Draguillo' means the *little* dragon tree, and it certainly has grown in the intervening years! Let's hope that all the names and initials carved into its trunk don't kill it off!

Below the tree, ignore the path off right (to Las Palmas). Follow the road to the left, beside stunning coastal scenery (Picnic 28b), to the seaside village of **Roque de las Bodegas** (**4h20min**), where the BUS STOP is on the seafront.

29 CHAMORGA • ROQUE BERMEJO • FARO DE ANAGA • TAFADA • CHAMORGA

Map on reverse of touring map   **Distance:** 7km/4.3mi; 3h35min

Grade: strenuous descent/ascent of 600m/1950ft; danger of vertigo. Those who suffer badly from vertigo will find the return path *impassable;* this can be avoided by returning along the outgoing path.

Equipment: walking boots, fleece, rain-/windproof, picnic, water, whistle

How to get there and return: 🚌 to/from Chamorga (or 🚐 247 from Santa Cruz to Chamorga at 07.30 *Sat only;* returns 16.30, 19.30)

Short walk: Chamorga — Tafada — Chamorga: 4.5km/2.6mi; 1h 55min. Moderate, with an ascent of 250m/820ft; equipment, access as main walk. Start the walk on the path across from the church. Ignore a fork off to the right at the outset. After about 10 minutes, follow the path round to the left (*do not* take the path straight ahead up the *barranco*). Your path bends back right and climbs the left-hand side of the *barranco*. Three minutes later, ignore a turn-off left for Cumbrilla. In another 20 minutes reach the Cabezo del Tejo/El Draguillo junction and turn right. Five minutes from the 'crossroads', after stunning cliff-top views, ignore a path descending to right. Keep left all the way along the top of the ridge to Tafada — a derelict building (1h20min). Here you join the main walk at the 3h-point. Chamorga lies 35 minutes away.

Alternative walk: Chamorga — Roque Bermejo — Faro de Anaga — El Draguillo — Roque de las Bodegas: 13km/8mi; 5h20min. Strenuous, with overall ascents of 400m/1300ft and descents of 950m/3100ft; you must be sure-footed and have a head for heights; danger of vertigo; equipment, access *by bus* as main walk; return on 🚐 246 from Roque de las Bodegas (as walk 28, page 127). This walk, somewhat easier than the main hike, visits some of the most spectacular scenery on Tenerife. Follow the main walk to the turn-off above the lighthouse (2h10min), where it leaves the main path to head up a crest to Tafada. Instead, keep straight along the main path. Ten minutes from the turn-off, come to a pleasant picnic spot, by a spring. Coming to an enormous rock with a wine press on the top, circle it to the right, then bear left to cross the *barranco* (please close the gate in the *barranco*). Ascending, you pass below Las Palmas (3h10min) and head along the sea-cliffs. A stiff ascent takes you up and across steep hillsides, covered in loose gravel, before you desend to El Draguillo (4h; photograph pages 32-33). From here take the road to Benijo, then the TF134 to Roque de las Bodegas, 1h10min away (see notes for Walk 28 and photograph on page 22).

Chamorga, a serene little village, beautifully sited in the isolated northeastern tip of the island, is where our hike begins and ends. From Chamorga we follow a narrow, shaded ravine that winds its way down to the idyllic bay of Roque Bermejo, only accessible on foot or by boat. An old lighthouse gives warning of Roque Bermejo — a sharp, reddish crag clinging onto the edge of the island far below. Rocky crests, with clear sea views down grassy slopes, return us to Chamorga.

Begin the walk in the village square at **Chamorga**. Just north of the church, fork right downhill on a path, passing a sign for 'ROQUE BERMEJO' in half a minute. Cane fills the moist valley floor. Five minutes along, you ascend to a track at the point where it narrows into a path. This path leads to the beach, without any turn-offs (although after half an hour you *may* have to deviate steeply down and back up, to round a landslide). A small stream idles its way down the ravine (**Barranco de Roque Bermejo**), replenishing the pools. A view of a faded-white house, set in the V of the *barranco,* is the first landmark as the ravine opens out to the nearby sea (**45min**). This is followed by Roque Bermejo, and shortly after, the lighthouse appears.

You reach a couple of old houses, joined together, overlooking the small basin shown below. Down in the ravine are tanks of water in store for the long dry summer and curtailing any would-be cascades. The basin, hemmed in by high escarpment walls, is a wealth of produce. To descend past these plots, turn left at the old building and make your way down the steep path. Take a deep breath and enjoy the scent from the Canarian lavender bushes.

A few minutes above Roque Bermejo, at a signposted intersection, turn right for 'BERMEJO' (**1h10min**). A few minutes downhill, you come to a small CHAPEL with a well-tended garden, and a large house with a tremendous view down into the bay. A sign indicates that this is the settlement of **Roque Bermejo**. The path at the right of the house leads to a small stony beach; the path between the chapel and the house goes to the port area, where you can swim from the steps of the quay. At the foot of Roque Bermejo sits a well-protected, crystal-clear pool set in the rocks. However, this is only accessible at low tide. The port area offers good bathing, however, for confident swimmers. This beautiful enclosed rocky bay is encircled by the sheer slopes that mark the end of the island.

Roque Bermejo, from the old houses near the 40min-point

Back at the junction, head straight up the wide old lighthouse path, signposted 'EL FARO, LAS PALMAS'. Bits and pieces of the path are gradually falling away. The **Faro de Anaga**, a good 20 minutes uphill, is a pleasant place to recuperate from the steep climb and take in the surroundings. The continuation of your path clambers over rock, to the left of the lighthouse. On the crest of the ridge, behind the lighthouse, the Roques de Anaga are visible.

Five minutes up from the lighthouse (a minute or two up the crest; **2h10min**), leave the main path and continue up a smaller path on the left, making for the crest above. This path heads straight up the ridge, so you can't go wrong. *(The main path continues to Las Palmas and is the route of the Alternative walk.)* Your route is up the very steep grassy slope; it affords good views over both sides of the lateral ridge as you ascend.

Eventually you leave the crest of the ridge and start moving inland, constantly climbing. As you rapidly gain height, the terrain becomes rockier and more sheer, with the possibility of vertigo for those unaccustomed to heights. Enormous *Aeoniums* plaster the bare rock faces. Heading round into an inner valley, the path passes above a natural balcony of rock — an excellent viewpoint for the Roques de Anaga. Not far above this, the path divides: both forks lead to Tafada. The left fork goes via the top of the crest, with spectacular views. **Tafada (3h)**, just a solitary stone farm building cradled in a dip in the ridge, makes a good viewing point. From here you look straight down into the Barranco de Roque Bermejo.

Continue up the left-hand side of the ridge, keeping left at the fork. Those who suffer from vertigo will find this path unnerving for a couple of minutes. As you round a crest two minutes later, the school — slightly apart from the rest of the village — comes into sight in the distance. At this point, the path begins descending a steep rock face. This is another place where *those prone to vertigo may well find themselves unable to continue.* There's a rickety piece of railing to help, *but don't lean on it!*

Less than 15 minutes from Tafada, you cross a crest and come upon a picture-postcard view of Chamorga (Picnic 29). On the descent, notice the 'dog's head'-rock at the end of this crest. Cumbrilla sits safely across the valley on a parallel ridge. A further 10 minutes down, you reach the first houses and a bar/shop in **Chamorga (3h 35min)**. Be sure to sample the superb local wine and goats' cheese.

30 IGUESTE • BARRANCO DE ZAPATA • PLAYA DE ANTEQUERA • BARRANCO DE ANTEQUERA • IGUESTE

Map on reverse of touring map   **Distance:** 10.5km/6.5mi; 5h35min

Grade: very strenuous, with total ascents/descents of over 900m/3000ft; you must be sure-footed and have a head for heights; danger of vertigo. *Recommended for experienced/adventurous walkers only.*

Equipment: walking boots, sunhat, fleece, rain-/windproof, walking stick(s), whistle, picnic, plenty of water

How to get there and return: 🚌 102 from Puerto to/from Santa Cruz (Timetable 1); journey time 1h; *change to* 🚌 245 to/from Igueste (Timetable 15); journey time 30min. Or 🚗 to/from Igueste

Short walks

1   **Igueste — 'Semáforo' — Igueste**: 6km/3.7mi; 2h10min. Strenuous ascent/descent of 400m/1300ft, but no danger of vertigo; equipment and access as main walk. Follow the main walk for 55min, then continue to the Semáforo, the old abandoned tower, for an excellent view over the Playa de Antequera. Return the same way.

2   **TF123 — Las Casillas — Igueste**: 5.5km/3.4mi; 2h15min. Easy, with a long descent of 600m/1970ft; equipment as main walk; access on 🚌 247 from Santa Cruz (Chamorga bus; departs 15.00 daily *except Sun;* ask to be dropped off at 'el camino para Las Casillas'; journey time 1h); return as main walk. The path begins where you leave the bus, just below a road forking right off the main TF123. Follow this well-worn path towards Las Casillas, ignoring all forks turning straight uphill or down. *Attention is needed* within the first 20 minutes, when you come to a fork as you ascend to the top of a crest: go *right* here, then head left to the top of the crest. Below the first house encountered, at a fork, climb uphill to the right. Las Casillas (Picnic 30b; photograph page 16) is reached in 30min. From the hamlet, initially veer left round the side of the ridge. Five minutes later the path takes you over the ridge, to descend the right-hand side. Some 15 minutes from Las Casillas, back on the top of the crest once more, you come to a junction (just beyond the last telephone pole). Head right here for Igueste. Five minutes later you pass a second path off to the left: here descend to the right, joining the main walk, which has climbed up from the Playa de Antequera. Pick up the main walk notes in the last paragraph on page 135.

P laya de Antequera lies in one of the most beautiful bays on Tenerife. The fact that it is only accessible by boat or on foot makes this tranquil little harbour even more special. The short walks make ideal early-evening excursions. The long bus journey to reach the starting point of Short walk 2 is an adventure in itself: the minibus twists and winds its way up and along the *cumbre* on a ribbon of road, tooting on every corner. If there's a cloudless sky, you'll be rewarded with unsurpassed views. By contrast, it's just a short coastal ride above small, sandy coves set in the cliffs to get to Igueste (de San Andrés), where the main walk and Short walk 1 begin. This proud little village, with its well-tended groves of mangoes, avocados, guavas and bananas, sits just up from the sea, inside the Barranco de Igueste. Stay on the bus to the end of the road, where the bus turns round.

Start out by following the paved path ('CASAS DE ABAJO') to the plaza in **Igueste**. Climb the steps behind the CHURCH, then turn left into the first alley (PASAJE JULIO). Take the first right turn and then the second left, to pass a tall TV mast and head towards the cemetery. After about 50m/yds go up steps that initially take you to the left, before turning right onto a slowly climbing footpath. Shortly afterwards, turn left on a beautiful old steeply rising path marked with a BLUE ARROW. You leave the village behind, heading towards an old tower. This tower ('Semáforo') was used before the days of radio, to send hand-signals. Chiselled out of the slope, the path climbs relentlessly. *Euphorbia,* various cacti, and bright green, drooping *valo,* with its soft, needle-like leaves, cover the hillside. White chrysanthemums are in full bloom in spring. A prominent rock, standing just off the path (**35min**), makes a good viewpoint over the coastline towards Santa Cruz.

Just before the path levels out (and immediately opposite a 6m/yd-long gap in the low man-made rock wall you have been following; **55min**), turn left inland (CAIRNS). *(But the Short walk continues straight on to the signal tower.)* Clamber over a rough, rocky trail to the crest of this ridge. On reaching the crest, continue to the left, to a derelict CHAPEL (**1h15min**). This is a lovely spot to take a break and feed the tame lizards! Igueste lies far below, set above the groves of fruit trees. **Montaña de Atalaya**, on your right, just a couple of minutes away (marked by a conspicuous white pillar), is the best spot for viewing Playa de Antequera. There's no path to the summit, but

Barranco de Igueste, from the road at the end of the walk

View back down over the Playa de Antequera from the return path.

the climb is very straightforward.

From the chapel continue along the path, crossing the crest. Ten minutes from the chapel, in the upper reaches of the **Barranco de Zapata**, strike off right towards the beach (**1h30min**). Your turn-off comes just after the path has levelled out; a small CAIRN marks the spot. Descending rapidly, you drop through the remains of old terraced plots into the valley below. The path is amply marked with SMALL CAIRNS. You first cross a GULLY, then scramble down to the riverbed, sometimes on all fours; follow the CAIRNS. You enter the RIVERBED at a junction of two *barrancos* and follow it for 80m/yds, until you can go no further. Then you have to scramble or pull yourself up onto the left bank, just above the drop into a DRY CASCADE (**1h55min**). From here on, you remain on the left side of the *barranco,* gradually ascending. Dark, gaping holes mark the hillsides. *Cardón* (see page 39) adds a touch of severity to the slopes. Another dry stream bed is crossed, then the path climbs again. Keep more or less level round the hillside. You pass a shepherd's shelter — a rocky overhang with the remains of a couple of small STONE PENS. Later the path heads below an impressive DYKE slicing its way seaward down the escarpment. Looking around the sheer hillside, you have a stunning view of the Playa de Antequera. Beyond the dyke, you head up a very steep and narrow goats' path — a vertiginous stretch, high above the sea, with sheer drops to the right. *Tabaiba* (page 92) and more brilliant green *valo* bushes (page 56) cover the slopes.

At the end of the ridge, overlooking the Barranco de Antequera, the path veers off down the nose of the ridge to **Playa de Antequera** (**2h45min**). Two lone dwellings sit in a gentle curve in the slopes above the beach, and a small harbourside building — long since abandoned — lies at the end of it.

Your return is via the **Barranco de Antequera**, directly behind you. Follow the path that climbs to the houses from the building at the harbour. Two minutes up, fork right on a path that ascends the hillside between the first house and a shed on the left, climbing above the second house. The path briefly follows a large WATER PIPE.

The Barranco de Antequera is every bit as dramatic as the Barranco de Zapata. Green-leafed *tabaiba* and curly-leafed sea lavender (page 56) illuminate the inclines with their brightness. A buttress of rock crowns the top of the ridge above you. Less than 15 minutes up, you round the nose of a ridge and have the spectacular view shown opposite, back down to the beach framed by the walls of the *barranco*. A few minutes later you cross the *barranco* — the first of many crossings. Your path ascends steadily; the vegetation thickens and soon swallows you up.

Ignore the faint fork off to the left (usually blocked off with stones) just before crossing the *barranco* for the sixth time. The valley has now become lush with greenery and, nearer the pass, large rosetted *Aeoniums,* perfectly circular, are plastered across the rock walls, interspersed with the clinging branches of chunky *candelabra.* Then, just before crossing the pass, you walk below a bare rock face.

Some 1h30min up from the beach you reach the PASS (**4h15min**), from where you look straight down into the Barranco de Igueste. The path continues up the crest, heading right, and then forks: go left here. Descending into the **Barranco de Igueste**, you soon notice the aroma of *Artemisia,* a green/grey-leafed plant. *Attention:* a minute further on, you pass beneath a POWER CABLE. A goats' path continues straight on here, but you scramble *uphill to the right,* across a rocky face with well-worn steps cut into it. This fork off takes you onto the LAS CASILLAS/IGUESTE PATH in three minutes. *(Short walk 2 joins here.)*

Here you descend to the left (PAINTED STONE MARKER). Ignore a faint fork off to the right about 18 minutes downhill. Just above the road you pass above a cottage and soon reach a fork. Descend to the left and meet the road (**5h10min**). Turn left and descend to **Igueste** (**5h35min**). There's a BUS STOP where you enter the village, or five minutes along to the left, where the bus turns round.

BUS TIMETABLES

Below is a list of destinations covered by the following pages of timetables, which give access to all the walks in the book. Numbers following place names are **timetable numbers**. There are more buses *and departures* than those listed here; see latest TITSA timetables (www.titsa.com).*

1 🚌 102: Puerto de la Cruz to Santa Cruz; EXPRESS; daily

Puerto	La Laguna	Santa Cruz	
07.15	08.00	08.10	*An even faster express bus service* (🚌 103) does not call at the airport or La Laguna. Departs from both Puerto and Santa Cruz *Mon-Fri* at 07.00, 08.00, 09.00, then runs half-hourly till 19.00, then 20.00, 21.00. On *Sat/Sun/hols* buses run hourly, departing Puerto from 09.00 till 21.00 and Santa Cruz from 08.50 till 19.50.
	then every 30 minutes until		
21.15	22.00	22.10	
Santa Cruz	**La Laguna**	**Puerto**	
07.00	07.15	07.55	
	then every 30 minutes until		
20.30	20.45	21.25	

2 🚌 345: Puerto de la Cruz to La Caldera; daily

Puerto	La Orotava	Aguamansa	La Caldera
07.00*	07.15*	07.45*	—
08.00*	08.15*	08.45*	—
08.45	09.00	09.30	09.45
	and approximately every 45 minutes until		
17.15	17.30	18.00	18.15
La Caldera	**Aguamansa**	**La Orotava**	**Puerto**
12.50	12.55	13.30	13.45
13.34	13.50	14.25	14.40
14.20	14.25	15.00	15.15
15.10	15.15	15.50	16.05
16.10	16.15	16.50	17.05
16.50	16.55	17.30	17.45
17.40	17.45	18.20	18.35
18.25	18.30	19.05	19.20
	19.20*	19.50*	20.05*

*terminates/starts out from Aguamansa; #only to La Orotava

3 🚌 350: Puerto de la Cruz to La Orotava; daily

Puerto	La Orotava		La Orotava	Puerto
07.00	07.15		07.30	07.45
and every hour until			*and every hour until*	
23.00	23.15		22.30	22.45

4 🚌 354: Puerto de la Cruz to Icod de los Vinos; daily

Puerto	Icod el Alto	La Guancha	Icod de los Vinos
07.30	08.05	08.15	08.30
	and every hour on the half hour until		
20.30	21.05	21.15	21.30
Icod de los Vinos	**La Guancha**	**Icod el Alto**	**Puerto**
08.00	08.15	08.25	09.00
	and every hour on the hour until		
19.00	19.15	19.25	20.00

*Some key words on Titsa timetables: *excepto* (not on); *sólo* (only on); *domingos* (Sun); *sábados* (Sat); *festivos* (holidays); *pasa por* (runs via); *salida* (departs from); *hasta* (goes to); *cada* (every)

5 🚌 348: Puerto de la Cruz to Las Cañadas; daily

Puerto (depart)	09.15	Parador (depart)	16.00
La Orotava	09.30	Teide cable car	16.05
El Portillo	10.15	Montaña Blanca	16.15
Visitors' Centre	10.17	Visitors' Centre	16.28
Montaña Blanca	10.50	El Portillo	16.30
Teide cable car	11.05	La Orotava	17.10
Parador	11.15	Puerto	17.30

6 🚌 363: Puerto de la Cruz to Buenavista; daily

Puerto	San Juan	Icod de los Vinos	Los Silos	Buenavista
06.00	06.20	06.45	07.15	07.20
		and every hour on the hour until		
21.00	21.20	21.45	22.15	22.20
Buenavista	Los Silos	Icod de los Vinos	San Juan	Puerto
06.30	06.35	07.05	07.30	07.50
		and every hour on the half hour until		
20.30*	20.35	21.05*	—	—

*the bus at 20.30 terminates at Icod de los Vinos; all others go through to Puerto

7 🚌 460: Icod de los Vinos to Playa de las Américas; daily

Icod	Erjos	San José turn-off	Guía de Isora	Playa Américas
07.30	08.05	08.10	08.45	09.15
10.00	10.35	10.40	11.15	11.45
12.00	12.35	12.40	13.15	13.45
14.05	14.40	14.45	15.20	15.50
16.00	16.35	16.40	17.15	17.45
18.00	18.35	18.40	19.15	19.45
20.10	20.45	20.50	21.25	21.55
Playa Américas	Guía de Isora	San José turn-off	Erjos	Icod
07.20	07.50	08.25	08.30	09.05
09.45	10.15	10.50	10.55	11.30
12.00	12.30	13.05	13.10	13.45
13.55	14.25	15.00	15.05	15.40
16.00	16.30	17.05	17.10	17.45
18.00	18.30	19.05	19.10	19.45
20.00	20.30	21.05	21.10	21.45

8 🚌 360: Icod de los Vinos to La Montañeta (San José bus); daily

Icod	La Montañeta	La Vega	La Montañeta	Icod
07.15	07.50		10.10	10.45
09.25	10.00	lies half-	12.15	12.50
11.30	12.05	way between	15.45	16.20
15.00	15.35	Icod and	19.10	19.45
18.30	19.05	La Montañeta	20.30	21.05

9 🚌 342: Playa de las Américas to Las Cañadas; daily

Playa de las Américas (depart)	09.15	El Portillo (depart)	15.15
Los Cristianos	09.30	Visitors' Centre	15.20
Arona	09.40	Montaña Blanca	15.30
Vilaflor	10.00	Teide cable car	15.40
Parador	11.00	Parador	16.00
Teide cable car	11.15	Vilaflor	17.00
Montaña Blanca	11.30	Arona	17.20
Visitors' Centre	11.40	Los Cristianos	17.30
El Portillo	11.45	Playa de las Américas	17.45

10 🚐 347: La Orotava to Realejo Alto; daily

La Orotava	Benijos	Palo Blanco	Cruz Santa	Realejo Alto
09.10	09.30	09.40	09.50	10.00
11.05	11.25	11.35	11.45	11.55
13.05	13.25	13.35	13.45	13.55
15.05	15.25	15.35	15.45	15.55
17.05	17.25	17.35	17.45	17.55
19.10	19.30	19.40	19.50	20.00
Realejo Alto	**Cruz Santa**	**Palo Blanco**	**Benijos**	**La Orotava**
10.05	10.15	10.25	10.35	10.55
12.05	12.15	12.25	12.35	12.55
14.05	14.15	14.25	14.35	14.55
16.05	16.15	16.25	16.35	16.55
18.05	18.15	18.25	18.35	18.55
20.05	20.15	20.25	20.35	20.55

11 🚐 366: Buenavista to Las Portelas; daily

Buenavista	El Palmar	Mondays to Fridays	El Palmar	Buenavista
07.30	07.45*		08.05#	08.20
09.30	09.45*		10.05#	10.20
13.15	13.30*		14.05#	14.20
17.30	17.45*		18.05#	18.20
19.30	19.45*		20.05#	20.20
07.30	07.45*	Sat, Sun/holidays	08.05#	08.20
11.30	11.45*		12.05#	12.20
13.30	13.45*		14.05#	14.20
15.15	15.30*		16.05#	16.20
19.30	19.45*		20.05#	20.20

*arrives La Montañeta 1min and Las Portelas 5min later; #departs Las Portelas 5min earlier

12 🚐 111: Santa Cruz to Playa de las Américas; daily

Santa Cruz	Candelaria	Poris de Abona	Los Cristianos	Playa Américas
		Mondays to Fridays		
06.00	06.15	06.50	07.25	07.30
		and every 30minutes until		
21.30	21.45	22.20	22.55	23.00
		Saturdays, Sundays and holidays		
06.30	06.45	07.20	07.55	08.00
		and every hour on the half hour until		
21.30	21.45	22.20	22.55	23.00
Playa Américas	**Los Cristianos**	**Poris de Abona**	**Candelaria**	**Santa Cruz**
		Mondays to Fridays		
06.00	06.05	06.40	07.15	07.30
		and every 30minutes until		
21.30	21.35	22.10	22.45	23.00
		Saturdays, Sundays and holidays		
06.30	06.35	07.10	07.45	08.00
		and every hour on the half hour until		
21.30	21.35	22.10	22.45	23.00

13 🚐 105: Santa Cruz to Punta del Hidalgo; daily

Santa Cruz	La Laguna	Tegueste	Bajamar	Punta Hidalgo
07.35	08.05	08.20	08.30	08.45
		and every 30min until		
19.35	20.05	20.20	20.30	20.45
Punta Hidalgo	**Bajamar**	**Tegueste**	**La Laguna**	**Santa Cruz**
08.00	08.10	08.25	08.40	09.10
		and every 30min until		
20.00	20.10	20.25	20.40	21.10

14 🚐 246: Santa Cruz to Almáciga/Roque de las Bodegas; daily

Santa Cruz	San Andrés	El Bailadero	Taganana	Almáciga
		Mondays to Fridays		
06.50	07.00	07.25	07.35	07.40
10.30	10.40	11.05	11.15	11.20
13.10	13.20	13.45	13.55	14.00
14.15	14.25	14.50	15.00	15.05
17.05	17.15	17.40	17.50	17.55
		Saturdays, Sundays and holidays		
07.05	07.15	07.40	07.50	07.55
09.10	09.20	09.45	09.55	10.00
11.40	11.50	12.15	12.25	12.30
14.15	14.25	14.50	15.00	15.05
17.05	17.15	17.40	17.50	17.55

Almáciga	Taganana	El Bailadero	San Andrés	Santa Cruz
		Mondays to Fridays		
14.20	14.25	14.35	15.00	15.10
15.30	15.35	15.45	16.10	16.20
18.10	18.15	18.25	18.50	19.00
20.25	20.30	20.40	21.05	21.15
		Saturdays, Sundays and holidays		
12.45	12.55	13.05	13.30	13.40
15.30	15.35	15.45	16.10	16.20
18.10	18.15	18.25	18.50	19.00
21.20	21.25	21.35	22.00	22.10

15 🚐 245: Santa Cruz to Igueste; daily

Santa Cruz	Igueste	*Mondays to Fridays*	Igueste	Santa Cruz
07.25	07.55		12.30	13.00
09.10	09.40		15.10	15.40
11.50	12.20		17.10	17.40
14.10	14.40		19.10	19.40
16.10	16.40		21.10	21.40
08.40	09.10	*Sat, Sun/holidays*	15.30	16.00
10.30	11.00		17.30	18.00
12.30	13.00		19.30	20.00
14.30	15.00		21.30	22.00

Departures from San Andrés about 15min after Santa Cruz (outbound) or Igueste (inbound)

16 🚐 325: Puerto de la Cruz to Los Gigantes; daily

Puerto	Erjos	Los Gigantes	Los Gigantes	Erjos	Puerto
08.40*	09.55*	10.25	08.40	09.10	10.25
10.35	11.50	12.25	10.55*	11.25	12.40
14.45	16.00	16.30	12.55	13.25	14.40
16.45*	18.00	18.30	17.15	17.45	19.30

*Mon-Fri only

17 🚐 075: La Laguna to Las Carboneras and Taborno; daily

La Laguna	Cruz del Carmen	Casa Carlos**	Las Carboneras	Taborno
		Mondays to Fridays		
06.45	07.05	07.10	07.40*	07.25*
09.15	09.35	09.40	10.10*	09.55*
13.05	13.25	13.30	13.45	14.00
15.15	15.35	15.40	15.55	16.10
		Sat, Sun/holidays		
07.30	07.50	07.55	08.25*	08.10*
16.05	16.25	16.30	17.00	16.45

*Calls at Taborno before Las Carboneras; **also called Cruce Las Carboneras

continues overleaf

Taborno	Las Carboneras	Casa Carlos**	Cruz del Carmen	La Laguna
07.45*	07.30*	08.00	08.05	08.25
10.00*	09.45*	10.15	10.20	10.40
14.00*	13.45*	14.15	14.20	14.40
16.15*	16.00*	16.30	16.35	16.55
19.30*	19.15*	19.45	19.50	20.10
		Sat, Sun/holidays		
08.10*	07.55*	08.25	08.30	08.50
17.00*	16.45*	17.15	17.20	17.40

*Departs Las Carboneras before calling at Taborno; **also called Cruce Las Carboneras

18 🚌 076: La Laguna to Afur and Roque Negro; daily**

La Laguna	Casa Carlos**	Casa Forestal	Roque Negro	Afur
		Mondays to Fridays		
06.55	07.20	07.45	08.00	08.10
13.15	13.40	14.05	14.20	14.30
16.05	16.30	16.55	17.10	17.20
19.00	19.25	19.50	20.05	20.15
		Sat, Sun/holidays		
07.00	07.25	07.50	08.05	08.15
13.15	13.40	14.05	14.20	14.30
16.25	16.50	17.15	17.30	17.50

Afur	Roque Negro	Casa Forestal*	Casa Carlos**	La Laguna
		Mondays to Fridays		
07.55	08.05	08.20	08.45	09.10
14.45	14.55	15.10	15.35	16.00
17.30	17.55	18.10	18.35	19.00
20.00	20.10	20.25***	20.50	21.15
		Sat, Sun/holidays		
08.00	08.10	08.25	08.50	09.15
14.45	14.55	15.10	15.35	16.00
17.45	17.55	18.10	18.35	19.00

*Also called 'Cruz de Taganana'; **also called Cruce Las Carboneras; ***this bus only stops here in summer

19 🚌 077: La Laguna to El Bailadero*; daily

La Laguna	Pico del Inglés**	Roque Negro**	Casa Forestal	El Bailadero
10.15	10.45	11.00	11.20	11.30
17.00***	17.30	17.45	18.05	18.15

El Bailadero	Casa Forestal	Roque Negro**	Pico del Inglés**	La Laguna
11.30	11.40	12.00	12.15	12.45
18.00****	18.10	18.30	18.45	19.15

*Also called 'Cruz de Taganana'; **turn-off to; ***18.00 Sat, Sun/holidays; ****19.15 Sat, Sun/holidays

20 🚌 073: La Laguna to Pico del Inglés

		Mondays to Fridays		
La Laguna	Pico del Inglés*		Pico del Inglés*	La Laguna
10.45	11.10		11.10	11.35
15.45	16.10		16.10	16.35
		Sat, Sun/holidays		
La Laguna	Pico del Inglés*		Pico del Inglés*	La Laguna
09.15	09.40		09.40	10.05
11.00	11.25		11.25	11.50

*turn-off to

☀ Index ―――――――――

Geographical names comprise the only entries in this index. For all other entries, see Contents, page 3. A page number in **bold type** indicates a photograph; a page number in *italic type* indicates a map (both may be in addition to a text reference on the same page. 'TM' refers to the large-scale walking map of the Anaga Peninsula on the reverse of the touring map. See also Timetable index, page 128. To save space, entries have been grouped under the following headings: Barranco (river or ravine), Choza (shelter), Faro (lighthouse), Galería (water gallery), Mirador (viewpoint), Montaña (mountain), Playa (beach), Punta (point) and Zona recreativa (picnic area with tables).

141